God's Pencils:
Christian
Parenting
and Teaching
in the
21st Century

God's Pencils: Christian Parenting and Teaching in the 21st Century

Arden Ruth De Vries Post, Ed.D.

For Barb
with many happy memories
of Stony Lake, Michigan

Arden Post
December 2002

CALVIN COLLEGE ALUMNI ASSOCIATION
GRAND RAPIDS, MICHIGAN

Calvin College Alumni Association, Grand Rapids, MI 49546

Library of Congress Control Number: 2001093818
        A catalog record for this book is available
        from the Library of Congress

Post, Arden Ruth De Vries
        God's Pencils: Christian Parenting and Teaching in the 21st Century

ISBN 0-9703693-5-2

Table of Contents

Developing Responsibility for Life and Learning

Facing Special Needs in Educating Children

Adjusting to Changes and Challenges in Family Life

Acknowledgements

Appreciation is expressed to Gordon Bordewyk, Editor, and Roger Schmurr, Assistant Editor, of *Christian Home and School* magazine for their editorial assistance over the years and to CSI for supporting our desire to publish a collection. Appreciation is also expressed to Henry Baron, professor of English, Emeritus, Calvin College, for his assistance in editing this collection, and to the Calvin College Alumni Association for their sponsorship of publications by faculty, and to Bob Alderink of the Calvin College Publishing Services who readily agreed to take on the design and lay-out of the book . Several Education Department student assistants contributed to the scanning of the original articles and to the revising and editing of the final manuscript: Matt Plantinga from Ontario, Canada, David Brasser from Grand Rapids, Michigan, Kellie De Witte from Hudsonville, Michigan, Jackie Eisenga from Cambria, Wisconsin, and Lindy McLean from Grand Haven, Michigan.

On a personal note, I express my deepest appreciation and love to my husband, John W. (Jack) Post, Jr. and to my children: Caroline Post Cone, Janine Post-Anderle, and John W. Post, III. Jack, Caroline, Janine, and John have not only put up with a wife-mother-teacher, but have graciously permitted me to share personal experiences. My grandchildren—Courtney, Tanner, and Carli Cone; Micah, Evangeline, and Sophia Anderle; and Simon and Samuel Post—have made their own contributions to this collection by providing ideas and photos to enhance the written word. And if those in heaven can look down, I want to thank my parents, Ann and Wilbur S. DeVries, for instilling in me the love of learning and sacrificing to provide me with Christian schooling for most of my education.

Introduction

"WE ARE ALL PENCILS IN THE HAND OF GOD"

So declared a bulletin board in a Christian School in Cambridge, Ontario, Canada.

Waiting for the beginning of a teacher professional day at the school, I reflected on the simplicity, yet profundity, of this statement and thought, "Yes. This statement sums up the role of Christians in the world today. As pencils inscribe a paper, we—parents, children, teachers, churches, and communities—must inscribe God's teachings on our world. To do so, we must seek to be God's servants and transform the world for him. All of us—children, teachers, parents, church, and community members—are God's pencils, his instruments, for doing his work in his world." In fact, it was Mother Teresa, founder of the Missionaries of Charity in Calcutta, India, and former high school principal, who told Christians everywhere, "We are all little pencils in the hands of God, writing his love letters to the world."

How do we get started along this lifelong journey of transforming the world for Christ? Parents are the first and most important instruments: we are the first "pencils" in our children's lives. Remember those first pencils we used in learning to write— those thick, sturdy, solid ones that leave a dark imprint on paper? Well, as parents we are like those beginning pencils we used as writing instruments. We are the most important instruments in our children's lives initially, a steady and sturdy force directing their development. We attempt to "write the script" for our young children. We give them their start and steer their lives in their formative years. Our task of parenting is both the greatest gift and the greatest challenge God gives us to do in our lives. We are God's writing instruments, and parenting is our major thesis! As a pencil inscribes the written page, so we, parents, inscribe God's ways of thinking and living on our children's hearts so that they, too, will become his instruments, imprinting his will on the world.

No One Said It Was Easy

As Christian parents, we covenant with God to bring up our children in the ways of the Lord. Through the teachings of the Bible, daily prayer, church instruction, and school involvement, we ask God to give us knowledge and wisdom in our parenting. To assist us in our quest, God provides Christian friends and family, as well as church and school communities, with whom we discuss the practical issues that arise. We reach out to others for help and suggestions. We take their ideas and experiences and formulate the practices that work best for our own families. Our common concerns lead us to value the experiences, ideas, and suggestions from others, because they have dealt with, or are presently dealing with similar issues in raising and educating children. Those with whom we consult are God's pencils as well, "writing" their ideas on our hearts so we can learn from them.

As my own children were growing up and as I taught future teachers at Calvin College, Grand Rapids, Michigan for sixteen years, the common concerns of parents became evident to me and often led me to write an article for a journal. Again, the pencil analogy fits here in a similar way. Just as God asks us to inscribe his ways on our children's hearts, so he, too, laid a burden on my heart to share my own experiences, and the experiences of so many others, with the vast audience of Christian parents. He led me to take pencil to paper and share stories, thoughts, and suggestions as one Christian parent and teacher to others. The articles contained in this collection are modified and updated from articles I published in *Christian Home and School* magazine, a publication of Christian Schools International. *Christian Home and School* magazine is specifically designed for Christian parents and teachers and features a variety of articles on topics of relevance to contemporary Christian parenting and teaching of children. Over the years, I was privileged to contribute the articles that have now become this collection, *God's Pencils: Christian Parenting and Teaching in the 21st Century*. The Calvin College Alumni Association, with the assistance of the Calvin College Publishing Services, has enthusiastically endorsed this publication with the prayer that it will be helpful to contemporary Christian parents and grandparents, church and community members.

Although the articles were originally published in a parenting magazine directed at Christian school parents, the articles deal with common challenges all Christian parents face, whether their children attend Christian or public schools. It is my profound prayer that God will enable the words that I wrote in these articles to spark discussion among current parents and assist them in the daunting task of Christian parenting in the 21st Century.

Real Life Situations

Here are some of the questions raised by parents, grandparents, church members, and neighbors that served to inspire the articles contained in this collection.

- "What should we be doing to help our child develop literacy skills— listening, speaking, reading, and writing, and yet not be 'pushy'?"

- "How can I help my granddaughter through the heartbreak of rejection when she is not invited to a birthday party?"

- "How can we help our children at home with reading? When we say, 'Read to us', they read a line or two and then refuse to do anymore! Yet the teacher tells us to read with them at home!"

- "Should we give allowances or should children just ask us for funds when they need money? We have friends who give allowances to their children because it teaches them responsibility. We have other friends who believe children should ask for money so they can evaluate the worth of what the children propose to spend it on."

- "What if our child doesn't 'fit the norm', that is, what if he seems to be gifted? Or if she has a disability? How do we handle it and how do we help our children deal with their own uniqueness as well as the uniqueness of others?"

- "Our family is going through some changes. I guess my spouse would call them, 'challenges': we are moving to a new community, and at the same time our family is expanding while we are losing older family members. Tension exists!"

Six Sections Deal with Different Issues

This collection is divided into six sections, each of which contains four to six articles. The content of the sections roughly mirrors the six questions posed above. Section one deals with some early issues parents face: children's self-esteem and the development of literacy. Parents are their children's first teachers. They set the stage for feelings about self and create the environment for developing language. Parents continue to support these areas as children go through schooling.

The second section deals with issues of acceptance and rejection: something we all face at some time in our lives, but one that causes us great pain when observed in our children. Not being invited to a party, not making the team, being a newcomer in school, feeling unpopular or on "the outside" are painful experiences for the child and parents.

The third section targets the issues of literacy and learning at home during the school years. How can parents help with reading? Should they encourage or enforce a reading time? Is there any way to read with a child who balks at reading a page aloud?

This section also discusses the home-school relationship and ends with scenes from Christian School classrooms.

The fourth section focuses on developing responsibility for life and learning by discussing issues parents face in the "growing up years": whether to give allowances, how to develop responsibility, and the ever-present question of how, or even whether, to assist a child in studying.

Section five deals with special needs, in fact, it raises issues that many families will want to consider further if they see their child described somewhat in the articles. Giftedness, disability, learning and reading problems are discussed as they were found in actual children whom I knew.

Finally, section six looks at changes that affect family life. Some families may deal with all of the changes that are presented here at one time or another, whereas other families will be able to identify with one or two. In any event, all families will find the real life experiences interesting as they see ways of dealing with parenting challenges. The articles in this section include adopting a child, looking at the holidays through eyes of sadness, dealing with the loss of a dearly loved pet, providing activities for summer vacation, letting go of a college-age child, and moving to a new community.

Developing
Self-Esteem
and Literacy
in the
Early Years

"I am Lovable and Capable"

*"You are one of God's children,
created in his image, lovable and capable,
and I'm glad you're mine!"*

I'm pretty. I'm ugly. I'm a loser. I'm a winner. I'm stupid. I'm smart. I'm slow. I'm fast. I'm lovable. I'm unlovable. I'm successful. I'm a failure.

How would your son or daughter respond if asked to choose those sentences which describe him or her? Would the positive statements outweigh the negative ones?

In recent years educators have paid a great deal of attention to children's self-concepts because there is a direct relationship between self-concept and school success. Social learning theory referred to "success strivers" and "failure avoiders" in describing children's approaches to learning (Woolfolk, 1980). Success strivers expect to succeed because of their previous successes and feelings of adequacy. Failure avoiders expect to fail, based on past failures and their sense of inadequacy. Success strivers take risks in attempting new learning tasks; failure avoiders try to avoid situations in which they might fail. The old adage appears to ring true, "Success breeds success." More recently, the terms, "mastery-oriented," "failure-avoiding," and "failure-accepting," have been applied to students' beliefs about their ability and self-worth (Woolfolk, 1998; see also Covington, 1992).

But how does success relate to self-concept? Aren't some children just born successful: intelligent, good-looking, outgoing, and athletic?

To a certain extent, it does appear that some children have what it takes. They are attractive, bright, friendly, athletic. However, although it certainly helps to have these positive attributes, most of how we feel about ourselves comes from others around us. Do others emphasize our strengths or weaknesses? Do they encourage our abilities or remind us of our disabilities?

For the younger child, parents and teachers are the ones who do the most to shape self-concept. Peers enter the picture increasingly as the child gets older, but parents and teachers play the most important role in the early years. Achieving a feeling of success and self-worth at an early age can help children through learning or social difficulties later on.

Self-concept is an extremely important part of our children's lives. Many observers believe that feelings about self can determine what children think about themselves, what they do, and what they become—in other words, who they are! With such a powerful force acting in a child's life, parents and teachers must do all they can to shape this into a positive force.

Building Self-Concept

The following suggestions, however, go beyond building a positive self-concept. They also build a bond between parent and child which says, "You are one of God's children, created in his image, lovable and capable, and I'm glad you're mine!"

1. *Love your child, as he or she is, and communicate this love with words and without words.* Touch is a real human need, and pats, hugs, or smiles should never be stifled. Little notes tucked in the lunch bag or hung up in the child's room can be warm reminders of affection.

2. *Speak openly and honestly with your child.* Acknowledge any problems that exist, but try to work through them and never lose sight of the child's positive traits. Criticism should be directed at behavior, not at the child's worth as a human being.

3. *Listen to your child.* Communication is a two-way process. Don't feel as if you need to have an answer all the time. Often our children just want a listening ear and some understanding.

4. *Spend time with your child.* Trips and outings are great, but so are walks in the woods, building a doghouse together, cooking over the grill, playing board games and puzzles, and having informal chats.

5. *Help your son or daughter have many experiences with success.* These can be geared to each child's level of physical and mental development. Catching a ball, setting the table, reading a word or a book, or completing an assignment are just a few of the ways a child can demonstrate success.

6. *Maintain a sense of humor.* Milk will spill and carpets will get muddy, but life goes on. The catastrophes of today are often the substance of wonderful family stories of tomorrow.

7. *Encourage self-reliance and independence.* Responsibility helps a child feel grown up, realize his or her capabilities, and prepare for further challenges. Independence breeds a positive self-concept; dependence inhibits it.

8. *Set reasonable rules and limits.* However, be sure you are not asking more than the child can accomplish or remember. In other words, don't set the youngster up for failure.

These school posters show our importance in God's sight which parents can affirm in their children.

9. *Encourage your child to be a risk-taker.* Urge him or her to try new things and praise the effort, even if the results are less than spectacular.

10. *Appreciate your child's individual abilities.* They may not include beauty, brains, or athletic ability—those attributes typically valued in society today—but God has given each of us gifts. They may include a kind smile, a sweet spirit, a helpful attitude, or maximum effort in spite of a disability. Each of us is God's workmanship—a unique creation!

11. *Establish realistic goals and expectations.* Don't necessarily expect your son or daughter to do all that you did and be all that you are.

Positive statements can reinforce your child's sense of self-worth. Don't use them only to recognize great achievement—that's easy. Instead, show sincere appreciation for your child's efforts when he or she didn't win the race, didn't receive the best grade on a paper, or didn't get elected class president. Here are some statements gleaned from parents:

> That kind of work makes me happy!
> You're very good at that! Nice job!
> Good going!
> Thanks for helping me! I knew you could do it! You did it that time!
> That's quite an improvement! Now you've figured it out!
> Now that's what I call a fine job! Keep it up!
> I like that!

> That's coming along nicely! I'm proud of you!
> I appreciate your effort! You're a great kid!
> I love you!

Your goal should be a child who can say, "I am lovable and capable." As Christian parents and teachers, we also want the child to add, "because God made me in his image to do his will for his purpose."

Kids' Poems Promote Self-Esteem

These creative writing efforts were produced by fourth grade students in Lenore Klunder's class at Ada Christian School in Ada, Michigan. The children were asked to tell about themselves, their feelings, and their personal qualities, emphasizing their assets.*

> Brandon is my real name.
> Running is fun.
> Always joking around.
> Nothing I can't do.
> Dinosaurs are my thing.
> On top of things.
> Never gives up.
>
> *B. J. Wong*

> Jonathan
> blissful, handsome
> I like to ski a lot.
> Sometimes I'm happy; other times I'm not.
> Nice kid!
>
> *Jonathan Doherty*

> Me
> I'm very bright.
> I'm spirited, sportive
> Someways, I'm unresponsible. Pretty.
>
> *Amanda Danforth*

I am joyful and playful, sometimes cheerful, happy, or sad. I like to be active outside and I like handwriting. I am good in it. I like math, spelling, creative writing, and Bible. Sometimes I have bad feelings and sometimes happy ones.

Anna Nielsen

---

*Parental permission granted when article was published in Christian Home and School *magazine.*

The Self-Esteem Credo — Art Fettig

God made me—I was no accident
No happenstance. I was in God's plan
And he doesn't make junk, ever.
I was born to be
A successful human being.
I am somebody special, unique,
Definitely one of a kind,
And I love me.
That is essential so that
I might love you too.
I have talents, potentials, yes,
There is greatness in me, and
If I harness that specialness,
Then I will write my name
In the sands of time with my deeds.
Yes, I must work harder, longer,
With greater drive,
If I am to excel,
And I will pay that price,
For talents demand daily care
And honing.
I was born in God's image
And likeness
And I will strive to do
God's will.

Art Fettig is a Christian author and lecturer who has devoted much of his work to promoting a positive self-concept in children. He is president of Growth Unlimited, Inc., of Battle Creek, Michigan. This verse, copyright 1980, is reprinted with permission.

Illustration by Patricia Ryan, ©1975 Argus Communications, used by permission.

Listening:
The First Step
Toward Language

"Listening to sounds in the environment and distinguishing among them form the basis for a child's first introduction to the world of language."

Sounds can be loud or soft, pleasant or irritating, like the ones in this excerpt from "Louder Than a Clap of Thunder" by Jack Prelutsky:

> Louder than an earthquake rumbles,
> louder than a tidal wave,
> louder than an ogre grumbles
> as he stumbles through his cave,
> louder than stampeding cattle,
> louder than a cannon roars,
> louder than a giant's rattle,
> that's how loud my father SNORES!
>
> (Prelutsky, 1984, p. 36. Quoted with permission from Harper Collins, 2001.)

Listening to sounds in the environment and distinguishing among them form the basis for a child's first introduction to the world of language.

Educators often speak of the pyramid of language when describing the components of language and the natural progression in language acquisition of the developing child. At the base of the pyramid is listening, the first component of language to which a child is exposed. At birth, children begin hearing the world around them, including the voices of others and their own. Speaking develops as young children attempt to communicate with those around them and imitate the sounds of their world and the words of others. Reading and writing follow listening and speaking. Educators and researchers have come to realize the crucial role that early experiences with listening and speaking play in later years when a child begins to read and write.

The pyramid of language has important implications for parents. We know that parents are the first and most important teachers of language for their young children and can do much to help their children develop language skills. You have only to listen to a toddler to pick up elements of a parent's speech: the choice of words, a regional accent, inflectional tone, and so on. I don't want to sound an alarm that sends parents scurrying to examine their grammar and speech patterns. For example, my own children may have picked up traces of my New Jersey accent, and this did not harm them (I hope). Of more importance than a standard dialect or correct grammar for children is the simple opportunity to engage in language interaction with their parents.

We live in a world of many sounds, and children learn to distinguish among the different sounds they hear. A young child

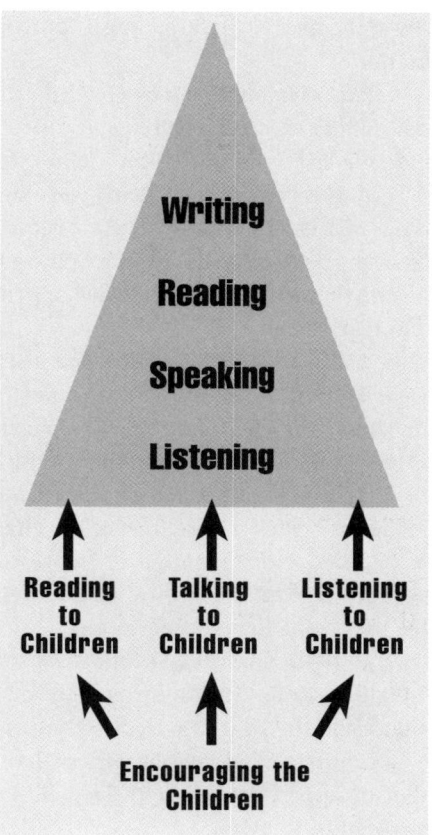

The Pyramid of Language

can differentiate between a parent's voice and the voice of a stranger. A kindergartner learns to differentiate among similar consonant sounds such as *p* and *b*. Children learn to attend to some sounds and ignore others. (Many parents and teachers realize this all too well!) In school, children must learn to pay attention to the teacher and ignore the background noise.

Encouraging Good Listening Habits

While many listening experiences occur as a natural part of a child's environment, here are some specific ways to encourage good listening habits.

1. *Ask children to name sounds they hear, particularly when the source of the sound cannot be seen.* "I hear a sound coming from up in that tree. What do you think it is?"

2. *Discuss how the source of the sound could be determined.* "How can you tell that the sound is a bird chirping?"

3. *Identify specific sounds with descriptive words that expand upon the iden-*

tity of the source: "barking dog," "growling bear," "running water," "hissing kettle."

4. *Play rhyming games by giving the first line of a rhyme or poem and asking the child to say the second line.* An easier variation is to have the child provide the last word of the line: "One two, buckle my _____"

5. *Play a "Guess the Sound" game by putting some objects in various-size boxes and having children guess what is in them.* The child with the correct answer gets to keep the object. Some good objects to use for boxes include: M & M's, pennies, marshmallows, pencils, crayons, a small pad of paper, and marbles.

6. *Listen to records or tapes and discuss how the music makes you feel or what mood the music creates.* Some musical compositions use different sounds to convey the idea of animals or objects. In *Peter and the Wolf*, for example, various instruments mimic the sounds of animals in the story.

7. *Listen to poems and stories on tapes or records.* Talk about how the reader indicates the feelings of the characters or the mood of the story.

8. *Play with language in interesting ways.* "The jackhammer says gggggggnrrrrzzzzzzzzzttttttt" (onomatopoeia). "Tommy the turtle touched his toes two times" (alliteration).

9. *Practice following directions by starting with one simple command and adding on to it.* "Please bring Daddy his snack." "Please bring Daddy his snack and then get him the newspaper."

Of course, we should be sure to thank the child, letting him or her know that we appreciate the help. The child may also enjoy giving directions for a parent to follow.

10. *Identify words or sounds that start the same, sound the same, or end the same:* "What word sounds like cat?" Or, "I have an apple. I wonder what other words start with that sound."

11. *Do clapping or tapping patterns similar to "Pat-a-cake" which many parents do with an infant.* An older child can imitate the parent's clapping pattern, then initiate one and have the parent be the imitator. Closing one's eyes enhances the concentration necessary to imitate.

Clapping the rhythm of a song without singing it can turn into a guessing game about which song has that rhythm. Early elementary children often learn to hear the number of syllables in a word by clapping out the sound parts.

12. *Talk, talk, talk, and involve the child in conversation about objects and events in his or her daily life.*

13. *Sing songs with or without musical accompaniment.* Parent and child can alternate singing lines of a familiar song. Parent: "Old MacDonald had a farm . . ." Child: "ee-i-ee-i-o!"

14. *Be a good listener.* Value what the child has to communicate and en-

courage his or her attempts. Some correction may be fine, but do not discourage the young talker. Also remember that many errors in speaking will correct themselves as the child grows and develops.

Parents are the child's first teachers. They initiate him or her into the world of language. By encouraging and fostering the development of listening skills, they are helping a child take the first step on the language pyramid, a step that will foster success in other areas of use.

One parent expressed her thoughts about listening with a poem.

Listen to the buzzing bee
Listen to the rustling tree
Listen to the words I speak.
Listen, child, to the world you seek.
Listening will be the key
To language yet-to-be.
Listen, now, and you shall hear
Words and sounds upon your ear.

Listening to stories helps children develop listening skills.

"I Want 'Dis' Dog": A Child Speaks

"From cooing and babbling to simple sentences and chattering, a child learns to master her world through speech."

Listening is the first component of language in which a child is involved. There are many things you can do to develop listening skills in your child and to prepare her for listening in a school situation. Speaking is a natural counterpart to listening. Through listening a child hears sounds and voices in the environment which become the impetus for making sounds and saying words of her own.

Three-year-old Nicole was visiting our house one day when she decided that she wanted a dog. She had been playing with our dog, Buffy, for several hours when she approached her father and said, "I want doggie."

Young children like to interact with animals, and this little girl expresses her wish to take this cocker spaniel home.

16

"Shall we get you a doggie some day?" was Charlie's reply.

"No!" Nicole answered emphatically.

Her puzzled father tried to sort this out, "I thought you just said you wanted a doggie, Nicole."

"I do!" Nicole insisted. "I want doggie!"

"Well, fine, as soon as Kylie gets a little older, we'll get a doggie!" Charlie answered.

"No, no," Nicole insisted, hugging Buffy tighter all the time. "I want Bussy! I want 'dis' dog!"

"Oh, I see," was her father's reply. "You want a dog *like* Buffy. Well, maybe someday Buffy will have puppies, and you can have one."

"No, don't want puppy. I want Bussy!" She was close to tears.

"You want Buffy—this doggie right here?" asked her dad.

"Yes," replied Nicole, happy at last that her father understood.

It took a lot of explaining to get Nicole to realize that "Bussy" was Janine's dog and had to remain in our house.

Language Development

While Nicole was conversing with her father, her one-year-old sister, Kylie, happily sat next to Nicole and Buffy, patting the dog and saying, "gog-gog." When Buffy walked around, Kylie followed chanting, "gog-gog." She was naming an object, and probably making a statement—"This is a dog." She continued to do this, occasionally stopping to tap her mom or dad while repeating "gog."

Nicole and Kylie demonstrate natural trends in children's language acquisition. In the first five or so years of life children do a tremendous amount of language learning. The cry which they produce at birth is soon supplemented with cooing and babbling. As children reach a few months of age, speech sounds begin to appear. They echo sounds in their environment, beginning a process of imitation that leads to speech production. By ten to twelve months, most children are saying a few simple words, as did Kylie. The term often applied to this stage of language development is *holophrastic speech,* in which a child uses one word to stand for a sentence or question. Kylie's "gog" stood for the sentence "This is a dog."

As children reach the age of two, two-word combinations are common. Two-year-olds seem to have their own ways of speaking and communicating. The term often applied to this type of language *is telegraphic speech* in which children use as few words as possible to telegraph meaning. Arnold Shapiro's poem "I Speak, I Say, I Talk" (1982), now published as *Mice Squeak, We Speak* in a book illustrated by Tomie dePaola (Puffin Books, 1997), indicates the excitement of a child learning to speak.

Cats purr.
Lions roar.
Owls hoot.
Bears snore.
Crickets creak.
Mice squeak.
Sheep baa.
But I SPEAK!

Monkeys chatter.
Cows moo.
Ducks quack.
Doves coo.
Pigs squeal.
Horses neigh.
Chickens cluck.
But I SAY.

Flies hum.
Dogs growl.
Bats screech.
Coyotes howl.
Frogs croak.
Parrots squack.
Bees buzz.
But I TALK.   Quoted with permission from World Books.

Between the ages of two and three, simple sentences are formed, and by the age of four to five the child is often referred to as a "grammarian," putting together some fairly complex sentences.

Assisting Language Development

A child acquires language through interaction with the environment. Nicole and Kylie were interacting with the dog, their parents, and the setting in which they found themselves. These situations are repeated dozens of times daily as children acquire language. While there are many naturally occurring situations in which language is tried, practiced, and used, there are several ways in which you can foster your child's language acquisition.

1. *Speak to the child.* The best type of oral interaction requires some response, such as a smile, a nod, a vocal sound, or an answer. The goal is to promote verbal interaction.

2. *Name objects around the house, the neighborhood, or the store.* Children's first words often name a person or object that is a significant part of their lives.

3. *Describe items or objects.* A favorite pet provides a good way to do this. For example, "Nicole, feel Buffy's fur. How does it feel? [It is soft and warm.]"

4. *Explain what you are doing as you are working around the house, driving in the car, or engaging in an activity.* Encourage the child to repeat a word or to name an object that is being used or observed.

5. *Include the child in conversations with adults or older children.* A simple question such as, "Shall we make a vanilla or chocolate cake?" or "What color shall we use to frost Grandma's birthday cake?" can help a younger child become involved.

6. *Permit children to greet visitors arriving at the home.* Young children also enjoy answering the phone, but be careful not to let callers struggle too long to make the purpose of their calls known to toddlers. Toy telephones are great for practicing, and the child can talk for an indefinite period of time.

7. *Give the child an opportunity to finish sentences* such as, "Today we went to the store and bought bread, and. . . . "

8. *Play time provides a natural opportunity to practice and develop language.* Children playing with friends or grown-ups will often pretend to take adult roles and imitate adult speech. My children and I often acted out such favorites as "The Three Little Pigs" and "The Billy Goats Gruff." I willingly became the wolf or the troll while my children engaged in a dialogue as pigs or goats or took turns serving as the narrator.

9. *Reciting poems, riddles, jingles, and songs enhances language development.* Making up a new line adds to the fun. Consider this dialogue:

Janine: "Little Miss Muffet
        Sat on a tuffet
        Eating her curds and whey
        Along came a spider
        And sat down beside her . . ."
Dad: "And said, 'Is this seat taken?'"
Janine: "No, Daddy. That's not how it goes!"
Dad: "Oh, no? How does it go?"
Janine: "And frightened Miss Muffet away."
Dad: "What's wrong with my line?"
Janine: "It doesn't *rhyme!*"

10. *Puppets, either purchased or homemade, enable a child to retell a story and to create the language to tell it in a personal way.* Children may also enjoy giving puppet shows for others.

11. *Artwork may become the source of speaking.* A child who has just painted a picture, sculpted an object, or cut and pasted a collage is usually delighted to explain it to interested adults or peers.

12. *Talking to a stuffed animal or doll is a natural way for children to prac-*

tice language. Even an imaginary friend, although sometimes a source of concern for parents, provides the child with a chance to use language.

13. *Time is probably the most important key to children's language development:* the natural passage of time during which the child grows, develops, and matures, as well as the time parents and others spend interacting with the child in listening and speaking.

Listening and speaking form a natural alliance. Although listening precedes speaking, it sets the stage and prepares children for using the language which they hear. By helping children develop listening skills and encouraging opportunities for speaking, parents are enabling children to climb the pyramid of language. Both listening and speaking become the foundation upon which reading and writing are built.

You Weren't Listening!
Untangling the Lines
of Communication

"Aw, you never listen to me.
You always figure I'm wrong.
You never listen to my side of the story."

"Mr. Stevens is a jerk," Joe shouted angrily as he made his grand entry to the kitchen, slamming the door and sending the dog skittering to safety.

"Joe! How many times must I tell you not to slam the door when you come home! Now march back outside and come in properly!" Mother saw the perfect opportunity to teach her son proper behavior.

"He gave me a detention for talking in class, and I wasn't even talking! He must be blind and deaf. I wasn't doing a thing, just staring at my text-book." Joe obviously hadn't heard Mother, or, if he had, he was plainly ignoring her.

"I can't hear a thing you say until you return to the door and close it quietly," Mother insisted.

"And then he had the nerve to give me an F on the test. I was sure I aced it, or at least got a B. He said my answers weren't complete enough. What a bunch of b-baloney!"

"Young man! What were you going to say?" At least Mother had forgotten about the door. "And you probably deserved the F *and* the detention." Apparently she had been listening after all! "If you act in school the way you do around the house, I can see why you got into trouble."

"Aw, you never listen to me. You always figure I'm wrong. It's 'Joe do this' and 'Joe do that.' You never listen to my side of the story. I'm going out!" And with that Joe left the house, slamming the door behind him.

"Now just a minute—" Mother said, but she was too late. Joe was running down the street toward his friend's house where he would find someone with whom he could commiserate and probably work off his anger in a game of basketball.

Joe's mother was left to think about the sequence of events and wonder what had gone wrong with her plans to greet her son cheerfully and ask about his day. The snack she had prepared for him remained untouched on the table.

Meanwhile Joe arrived at his friend's house. Steve greeted him, "Hey, man, what's the matter? You look ready to explode!"

"I am!" was Joe's response. "What a day! I failed the history test, and I got a detention for talking in class. And none of it was my fault. I think I'll change schools!"

"Good luck! I tried that last year, but my folks wouldn't hear of it! To them, the teachers can do no wrong, but wow, they think I do everything wrong!"

"You too? I thought I was the only one whose parents were always after him. Today when I came home, all my mom could say was 'Close the door quietly' and 'It's all your fault.'"

Conflicts in Communication

Every day in millions of homes, there are noisy confrontations between parents and children. Not only are these incidents common, but they are frustrating and upsetting. One mother said, "I'm becoming reluctant to be at home when my daughter gets home from school. I try to be pleasant, and I'm really glad to see her, but all she does is complain. By the time she goes to play with her friends, I'm completely depressed. And she insists on dumping her books all over the counter even though she knows that it gets on my nerves!"

Thomas Gordon in *Parent Effectiveness Training* (1975, 2000), offers several helpful suggestions for dealing with parent-child conflicts. He suggests differentiating between problems owned by the child and those owned by the parent. In the case of a child-owned problem, the child is prevented from satisfying a need, and the child's behavior is the child's problem. It is not a problem for the parent because the child's behavior doesn't interfere with the ability of the parent to satisfy his or her own needs. In the case of a parent-owned problem, the child is satisfying his or her needs, but the behavior interferes in some tangible way with the parent's ability to satisfy his or her own needs.

Some examples of child-owned problems include rejection by friends, failure to be chosen for a sports team, losing a game, poor grades, uncertainty about a future career, and concern about appearance, attractiveness, or dating. There is a tendency, according to Gordon, for parents to make many of these conflicts their own, which causes unnecessary grief for them and contributes to a deterioration of the parent-child relationship. Instead, parents should accept the fact that such problems belong to their children, and parental involvement should be caring, concerned, and helpful. This is not to suggest a hands-off policy, nor does it suggest taking over the problem and its solution. Instead, parents should accept the child's problem and

Roadblocks to Communication

Many comments frequently made by parents act as roadblocks to communication rather than providing a route for solving problems. The following are adapted from Gordon (1975, 2000):

1. *Ordering* – "Stop it right now!" "Tell your sister you're sorry!"
2. *Threatening* – "Watch out!" "The next time you…,you'll be sorry!"
3. *Preaching* – "I told you the glass would break!"
4. *Trying to solve* – "Just forget her, she's not worth it!" "Why don't you just find some other friends?"
5. *Lecturing* – "When I was your age, I had to…."
6. *Criticizing* – "How could you do something like that?"
7. *Ridiculing-* "Do you really want to go out looking like that?"
8. *Analyzing* – "I'll bet you talk a lot in class and that's why you got a detention!"
9. *Generalizing* – "All kids go through this sometime."
10. *Avoiding* – "You're always complaining! Let's talk about something else!"

trust the child to take an active part in its solution. Parents must practice active listening, avoid the typical roadblocks to communication, and demonstrate empathy, understanding, and genuine concern in order to help the child arrive at a solution.

Returning to the story of Joe's arrival from school, we see a common pattern of parental response. First, the mother orders him to close the door quietly, a reasonable request but one that totally ignores his agitated state. Her response suggests that she will pay attention to her son's feelings only after the door has been closed properly. Next he is admonished for almost saying a bad word, and his behavior at home and school is criticized. She also evaluates his behavior, concluding that it seems to lead to trouble.

I wonder what would have occurred if she had greeted his outburst by noting, "You are really upset! What happened?" Undoubtedly, Joe would have unloaded the same story. Suppose that the mom had then resisted the urge to order, admonish, or exhort, and in fact resisted the urge to say anything at all until her son finished his story. Then she could have said, "You really did have some problems! I'd be upset, too. Do you have any ideas on what to do about the F or the detention?"

It's likely that Joe would have responded, "There's nothing I can do!" Let's imagine the rest of the scene.

Mother: "Probably not, but it might help to talk to the teacher."

Joe: "Why? He's got it in for me!"

Mother: "Maybe he sees your behavior differently from the way you see it. I'd like to talk to him with you, and to find out about the test. He might have some ideas on studying."

Joe: "I don't think it'll do any good."

Mother: "Maybe not, but I'd like us to try for two reasons. First, I get upset when you come home so angry. Second, I'm afraid of cracks in the plaster or a broken window from the door slamming."

At this point Joe may or may not agree to a three-way conference. However, he might agree to confer with the teacher alone to work things out. If he refuses either a three-way or two-way conference, he could be encouraged to generate alternative solutions with the aim being to provide support and guidance for him to solve his problem.

But the after-school incident doesn't end here. There is also a parent-owned problem—the door slamming. While this seems to result directly from the child-owned, school-related problem, the door slamming seems to have bothered Joe's mother for some time, and, in Thomas Gordon's words, it keeps her from getting her needs met. What are her needs? Peace and quiet, preservation of the house, or other personal needs. Does active listening mean that this mom must forget about her own needs? Not at all! For a parent-owned problem, the I-message can lead to effective confrontation.

Consider what happened. Mother's overt or implied message was, "You are a bad boy for slamming the door and for getting the F and the detention. There is something wrong with you." An I-message accomplishes two things: First, it expresses the respondent's own feelings. Joe's mom might say, "I'm bothered by the door slamming. I'm worried about the house. I get upset about your problems." Second, this kind of message emphasizes the problem, attacking it and not the person. Mother may say, "I can't stand to have the door slammed. I want to help you settle the school matters."

A Problem-Solving Process

It can be difficult to distinguish between child-owned and parent-owned problems. In fact, many problems which arise are jointly owned or have no clear ownership. Active listening and using I-messages work well for any problem, as does following a clear process for problem-solving.

A six-step problem-solving process is as follows:

1. *Identify and define the problem.* This is necessary to make sure that everyone is focusing on the same issue. Joe could see the problem as the teacher's unfairness. His mother might see it as Joe's behavior. They need to settle what the problem really is before they can proceed.

2. *Generate alternative solutions.* This presents a real opportunity for active listening by everyone involved in the discussion.

3. *Evaluate the proposed solutions.* Which ones may be difficult to implement? Which are within the realm of possibility?

4. *Decide on the best solution.* Which one should be tried because it seems best or most acceptable to those involved?

5. *Work out ways to implement the solution.* Who does what? How will it be carried out? What needs to be done?

6. *Evaluate how the solution worked.* Did it accomplish the goal? Is the problem solved? Do we need to repeat or continue the solution? Should another alternative be tried?

This problem-solving approach may seem long and cumbersome. I have seen it work well but have also found the basic principles applicable to an abbreviated approach. Frequently I have talked with children and students in a manner similar to the following.

"So, what's the basic problem as you see it?" (I may also define how I see it and try to reach consensus.)

"What alternatives do you see?" (At this point I may make suggestions too.)

"When shall we get together again to evaluate our solution?" (Or, "let's talk next Friday afternoon.")

The value of active listening, using I-messages, and following a problem-solving process goes beyond the opportunity to have peaceful discussions instead of angry confrontations. These strategies of communication suggest the worth of the child created in God's image, the value of the child's input and opinions, and his ability to become involved in decision making. As Christian psychologist James Dobson has pointed out in his book, *Hide or Seek* (1979, 1999),and in much of his writing, parents have a tremendous influence on children's views of themselves. The quality of parent-child interaction influences the confidence with which children tackle problems and deal with pressures. A child who feels loved and respected, who has experienced adult support, who has been given a listening ear and a problem-solving guide, grows into adulthood feeling worthy and capable.

Interaction between child and adult is a two-way street. At times the parent may be in the driver's seat, but communication is a joint venture. One cannot help but be reminded of the biblical references to *communion,* the interaction of God and his people and the fellowship of the saints. Should we not also try for this spirit of communion in communicating with the children God has entrusted to us?

Circles on the Wall: A Young Child Begins to Write

"John was expressing a natural curiosity and interest in writing. Mother decided to set up a writing corner...."

"Who drew those circles on the wall?" asked Mother, trying to control her irritation. Two weeks of spring cleaning should have left the house free of excess dirt and marks for a while at least!

"Caroline did it," answered three-year-old John, somewhat sheepishly.

"That's funny," replied Mother. "They're written too low on the wall for Caroline's height. Besides, she has her own paper and workbooks to write in, so I doubt that she would write on the wall," she said more patiently, now that she was beginning to solve the mystery.

"Well, at least the marks are in chalk and should be easy to get off the wall," she continued. "I have a spray bottle and a cloth here for the first person who volunteers."

"I'll do it!" said John eagerly, and he grabbed the bottle and cloth and headed right for the circles on the wall.

When he returned, Mother said, "Thank you, John. Now I feel better. I like a clean and neat house, don't you?"

"I guess so," John answered. He was reaching for a pencil on the table.

"Writing is fun," Mother said.

"Yes!" said John. "And I'm learning to write just like Caroline!"

"Would you like some paper?"

"Yes," answered John, and he immediately began to draw circles.

"You make good circles," commented Mother. "Did you make those circles on the wall?"

John looked surprised that she had made the connection.

"I appreciate it that you were willing to clean them off the wall."

"I did it," John confessed and started to cry. Mother picked him up, hugged him, and had a little talk with him. She explained that lying was wrong, but writing was fine as long as it was done in the proper place. She explained that she could tell that John was sorry for writing on the wall. He had also made up for it by cleaning up. Then she went on to the hidden message in his actions. John was expressing a natural curiosity and interest in writing. Mother decided to set up a writing corner with lots of appropriate materials for a preschooler to use. She talked to him about where we can write and where we can't write. She gave him a small table and chair and equipped it with crayons, pencils, chalk, paper, a small chalkboard, and a magic slate. John was delighted and spent much time in his writing corner.

Mother also used other opportunities to respond to John's interest in writing. When they saw a hopscotch game which some children had drawn on a sidewalk, she asked John if he would like to draw one on their sidewalk. He took his chalk outside and was soon producing various pieces of "writing" and "drawing" on his own sidewalk. He was particularly delighted when his neighbor, Mrs. Brown, asked if he would like to inscribe something on her sidewalk, too.

The Development of Writing

John typifies a preschooler's emerging interest in the world of words. Children take their scribbles and early forms of writing seriously. Scribbling is the fountainhead for writing and occurs from the moment a child grasps and manipulates a writing tool (Vacca, Vacca, and Gove, 1987, 2000). Children typically move through several stages in their writing development.

The progression of children's early attempts at writing can be described by the following stages (Vacca, et al., 2000):

Early Scribbling—characterized by random marks on paper, occurring for many children by the age of one. These writing attempts resemble babbling in oral language development. Parents at this stage should encourage children to "write" (in proper places, of course) but refrain from pressuring the child to explain it.

Controlled Scribbling—characterized by systematic, repeated marks such as circles, vertical lines, dots, and squares, occurring typically between the ages of three and six. The scribbles usually strongly resemble the handwriting of the child's culture.

Name Scribbling—characterized by the child's realization that the scribbles mean something. They represent what the child wants to communicate. The speech-to-print match is being made, and the foundation is set for learning to read. At this point parents and teachers can engage in language activities in which the child dictates what he or she wants the adult to write. The child then "reads" his or her composition. At this stage the child continues to enjoy independent writing and often enjoys a combination of personal writing and a parent's writing. The following story by four-year-old Sean indicates how his mother encourages independent writing and also writes with him, recording his words and serving as a model.

Sean is saying—"One day there was Mrs. Post eating an orange and the peel is very good...."

Most parents are delighted when children show an interest in reading and writing. The early attempts at writing often produce "messages" in, on, or at surprising locations. Often a table, chair, refrigerator—in fact, almost any surface, vertical or horizontal—can become a target for the young child's eagerness to engage in self-expression. The common denominator for "pencil and paper" kids is a strong desire and need for self-expression and communication.

One day, Ther Was MISISPO
'OSH EAT A OrIG
iNThU PELEIs very
GOOD for you, and you put the other outside skin in the wastepaper canp, and the juice inside it is very yummy, juicy and sweet.

Fostering Writing Development

Here are some suggestions for parents who want to channel their budding young writer's enthusiasm into socially acceptable locations for that self-expression.

1. *Have a variety of writing materials available:* crayons and pencils (you may want to get some thick ones), paints and brushes, markers, and lots of paper. An old shirt serves well as a writing smock to protect clothing. It is especially appealing to children to have their own writing corner, as John did. An alternative is to have a small suitcase in which the child can store writing materials and use them when and where it is convenient.

2. *Chalkboards can be fun.* They vary in size from those on a standing frame to small lap-size tablets about the size of notebooks. In addition to writing with chalk, children can write with a paintbrush and water or trace over chalk writing with a finger.

3. *Fold several sheets of paper in half to make small books in which children can write and draw.* Assist them in writing their names on the cover to personalize them. These can be stapled or sewn in the middle to produce a binding. They work well for language experience stories too, in which an adult writes the words dictated by the child, leaving room on each page for the child to make the illustrations.

4. *Magic slates allow the child to write and erase.* Slates can also be made from any plastic lid, written on with a crayon, and erased with an old sock.

5. *Textured writing can be done by placing paper over sandpaper and writing on it with a crayon.* Children get the feel of letters and shapes when they trace their creations with a finger.

6. *A sandbox tray is a fun place to write and draw, using a finger or a stick.* A sweep of the hand produces a clean writing surface.

7. *An easel and poster paint allow children to experiment with color as well as with writing and drawing.*

8. *Pipe cleaners, clay, and modeling dough (such as Play-Doh) provide alternate ways to form letters and shapes.* This is also good for developing fine motor coordination.

9. *Fingerpaints provide the opportunity to write and draw, using fingers or sticks.* Be sure to have some soap and water nearby!

10. *Old wallpaper books and used greeting cards can be cut up to make new cards and stationery.* Children enjoy making them and writing or drawing

Matthew's first letter, with Mother acting as scribe.

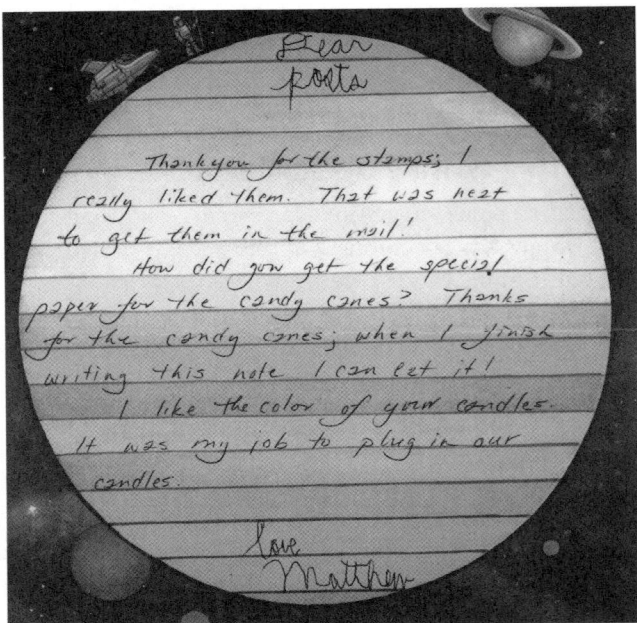

their own greetings inside. Grandparents and friends enjoy receiving them and should be encouraged to respond. The child then begins to understand the reading-writing connection as part of the communication process. The letter from Matthew, in which his mother served as scribe for the body of the letter, shows a child's beginning interest in correspondence.

The following letter written entirely by Matthew occurred six months later.

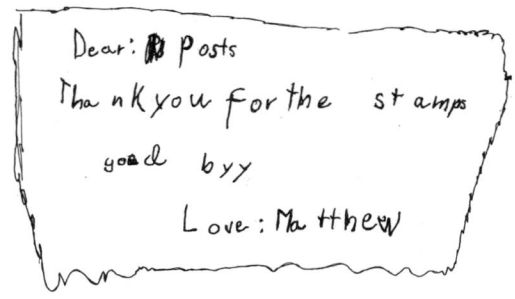

Today the ease of e-mail facilitates communication and saves postage. Children may enjoy dictating a message to a parent or older sibling to send to a relative or friend. As children get older, they can send their own messages. Young children may like to "type a message" even before they can actually "write" like the one I received from Micah. Later, he said to me, "Grandma Arden, I sent you a message. What does it say?"

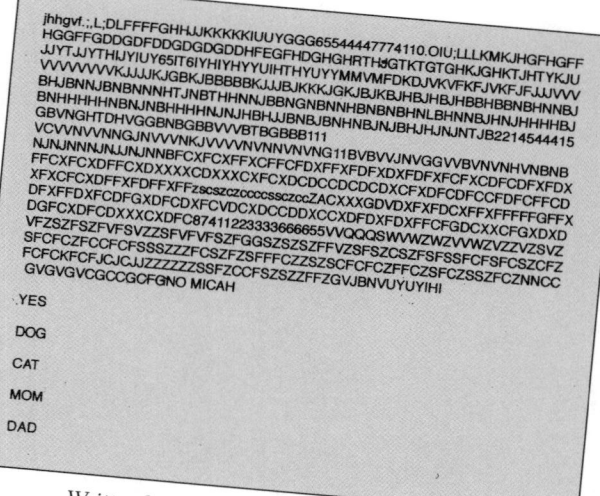

Written by Micah B. Post Anderle at age 4 1/2.

The possibilities for encouraging a young writer's efforts and enthusiasm seem endless. The parent is rewarded with a child who is proud of his or her work and who has a valuable start on the road to learning.

Helping Children Face Issues of Acceptance

Why Wasn't I Invited?
The Birthday Party
Tragedy

"The invitation said,
'Come to a Birthday Party!'
But of the fourteen girls in sixth grade,
only twelve were invited."

It happened again. Perhaps I should be used to it after all these years as a teacher and a parent. Perhaps you never get used to it. It cuts to the very core of my being. And it evokes very strong emotions: hurting for the one who is hurt, painfully recalling past rejection, suffering with the suffering one in whose shoes I once walked and in whose shoes many still walk each day at school.

What is this painful event, this source of grief and tears for so many school-age children? It is the annual birthday party, a time of fun, celebration, laughter, and games—unless you are the one who is not invited. The invitation to a birthday party signals anticipation of the celebration and acceptance in the world of the celebrant—for those who are invited. But it can also produce a feeling of rejection for the "outsiders," those who don't get asked.

A few years ago an elementary student entered my remedial reading session, looking dejected and downcast. All of my attempts to interest her in the lesson failed. I sensed there were more pressing matters to deal with, so I asked, "Kim, is there something I can help you with?" Immediately, she burst into tears.

"Jeannie is having a birthday party. She passed out invitations today. Everybody got one except me and Carla, just like last year! Now everybody is gonna talk about the party all week and all the fun they're gonna have. I wish I could stay home till the party is over!"

I felt like crying too, and the tears in my eyes must have conveyed my feelings. What was there to say to her?

Lots of stock phrases passed through my mind. I thought, "There will be other parties," but I knew Kim wouldn't be invited to those either if past practices continued. I could have said, 'Well, Kim, you know that I like you. You're a lovely girl, sweet and sensitive," and it would have been true, but it would have been little comfort to a girl rejected by peers.

Another response would have been to analyze the situation, asking as kindly as possible, "Why do you think you weren't included?" But that would have just accentuated a situation that both she and I knew existed. Kim was small and shy in a class of preadolescent girls who were developing physically and socially. Besides, Kim was from a poorer family than her classmates, and her clothes didn't stand a chance of competing with the latest styles and fads. I could have told her that these things don't really matter, that character and spiritual maturity are more important than being in style, but in her daily world, clothes, friends, and parties *did* matter.

I realized why I felt speechless and unable to offer the right words. It was because the situation wasn't Kim's fault, and there was nothing she could do about it. It was to others that I needed to speak, and that same afternoon the opportunity presented itself.

Jeannie, whose annual party caused Kim such grief, was a remedial reader who received help from me also. She arrived exuberantly, waving to her friends as they went on to other classes. She was bubbling with excitement and needed little prompting to tell me in great detail about the party plans. This was going to be her best party ever: first, bowling; then, out for pizza; and finally, a sleep-over.

"Why wasn't Kim invited?" I asked. Jeannie looked puzzled as if wondering why I would even ask.

"Well, why should I? Mom said I could invite the girls I want to, and Kim wasn't one of them. I can't have *everybody*, you know!"

"I understand that you can't have too many people, but two more, when you already have twelve, wouldn't be too many, would it? After all," I continued, "some parties have only five or six guests, and that makes sense to me. But when you invite twelve out of fourteen, I really feel sorry for the two who aren't included. You can imagine how they feel!"

"Oh, well, they wouldn't fit in anyway. They don't belong. I honestly don't think they'd be happy coming to the party." Jeannie sounded as if she were trying to convince herself.

"They certainly aren't happy by not coming," I replied. "Have you seen Kim today?"

"Oh, sure, she sits next to me in homeroom. She just sat there as quiet as usual." Jeannie seemed unable to identify with Kim's feelings and unwilling to try.

The next opportunity I had to talk to someone about the party seemed

Parties are fun… when you're invited!

almost too good to be true. Jeannie's mother came to school that day. She was a volunteer aide for one of the classes, and she came to school twice a week. Since she often spoke with me, it was easy for me to bring up the topic of the birthday party. I mentioned Jeannie's excitement and asked if she knew that two girls hadn't been invited. She replied, "Sure, I suppose there are always some who are left out. After all, you can't have everyone, you know!" She sounded like Jeannie. "I try not to get involved with the guest list. It's her party, and she can invite whomever she wants. It's only natural that she'll invite her friends!"

I had reached a dead end. The perpetrators of the birthday party seemed unable to look beyond their own interests, and the victims were left to suffer alone.

It was difficult to believe that any malice was intended. In fact, neither Jeannie nor her mother purposely set out to cause hurt feelings. Rather, they were just intensely involved in their own concerns and their own happiness. They were either unable or unwilling to see how their plans affected others.

The true tragedy of Jeannie's birthday party is that it is repeated in schools all across the continent. Christian schools are not exempt. The special tragedy for Christian schools is that we teach the love of Jesus for all his children and his compassion for the loved and unloved, the worthy and the unworthy. Yet the birthday party tragedy is just one way in which many of us fall far short of following his example.

What can we do as Christian parents and teachers to prevent the birthday party tragedy? Here are some suggestions.

Suggestions for Parents

1. *Don't let children invite almost everyone.* Check the guest list. Make sure that a few are not singled out to be excluded.

2. *When you can't have all the girls or all the boys in the class, or the whole class, have a few close friends,* say four girls out of a class of twelve girls, or six children from a class of twenty. Also be sure to send invitations by mail; it's impossible to keep invitations secret at school.

3. *Try making a general invitation to the class:* "Anyone is invited to stop by our house for cake and ice cream Friday night at 8:00." Not everyone will come, but at least they haven't purposely been omitted. My experience is that about half will show up. You can still take a few close friends out for dinner before the group arrives.

4. *If everyone isn't invited, schedule parties at a time when the invitees don't have to get on the bus carrying presents and sleeping bags,* thus accentuating the party. Have them arrive in the evening or on a Saturday afternoon.

Suggestions for Teachers

1. *Watch for party invitations being handed out and for those who are excluded.* Call the parent when only one or two students seem to be left out. The parent may not be aware of what has occurred. Be a special friend to the child who suffers from exclusion.

2. *For parents whose response resembles that of Jeannie's mother, tell them what you've observed over the years, and gently explain the tremendous hurt experienced by those who are excluded.*

3. *Consider making a general statement to parents at the beginning of the school year about parties, using an example such as Kim's and the suggestions given in this article.* Perhaps the message can be included in a September letter to parents.

4. *Encourage class celebrations of birthdays, whether or not parents are able to provide a treat.* One elementary teacher gives the birthday child a privileged position in the classroom for the day and provides a treasure chest from which the child chooses a gift.

For all of us, remembering when we, too, were left out is a first step in helping our children become sensitive to the needs of others. All of us have been excluded at one time or another, and we should commit ourselves to doing unto others as we would have them do to us. The birthday party tragedy is avoidable; let's eradicate it.

"I Didn't Make the Team" (and Other Losses)

*"Amy put on a brave face at school.
She congratulated the team members
and assured them she didn't care
that she hadn't made the team."*

It was a crisp, autumn day. Summer vacation was over, and teachers and students had returned to Centerville Christian High School anticipating a new school year.

Basketball Tryouts

"Girls' basketball team practice and tryouts begin tonight at 5:00 P.M. All interested girls should plan on a practice each night this week for one hour. Next Monday and Tuesday, same time, we'll have tryouts," came the announcement during homeroom.

"Are you trying out?" asked Amy.

"I'm not very good, but I'd love to be on the team," responded Jackie.

"Oh, but you are good! I saw you shooting free throws in P.E. yesterday," exclaimed Amy.

"I suppose it wouldn't hurt to try out. If I make it, fine. If I don't, who cares?" declared Jackie.

"That's exactly the way I feel," said Amy. "It's no big deal. But did you see the assistant coach? He's new this year, and he's so—oh, you know!"

"I'll bet half of the girls try out just because of him. Is that why you're trying out?" asked Jackie.

"Of course not. Let's say he's just an added attraction."

Amy and Jackie attended the practices and tryouts. They got new shoes, even though Amy's mother wondered why they had to buy equipment, as she called it, before they knew if Amy would make the team. "But, Mom, how can I play if I don't have decent shoes!" cried an exasperated Amy.

Team sports are great—but first you have to make the team! Amy would be watching from the bleachers . . . she didn't make the team.

"Besides, fifteen girls will be chosen, and only eighteen are trying out. The odds are pretty good that I'll make the team!"

On Wednesday morning the girls arrived at school early to read the team roster.

Amy scanned the list, then began to reread it more closely, just as Jackie shouted, "I made it! Oh, I can't believe it. I never thought I had a chance—all those good players! Can you believe it, Amy, I. . . . What's the matter?"

"I didn't make it," sobbed Amy as she ran to the girls' room.

Later in homeroom, Jackie noticed Miss Carter, the basketball coach, asking Amy to step out into the hall.

"Amy, I tried to call you last night, but no one was home," said Miss Carter. "I'm so sorry you had to find out this way. I really wanted you on the team, but I have only fifteen uniforms and couldn't take everyone. I'm sorry."

"That's okay," responded Amy. "It's no big deal."

Amy put on a brave face at school. She congratulated the team members and assured them she didn't care that she hadn't made the team. "I'm so busy, I don't know how I would have found time for it anyway," she rationalized.

But when she got home after school, her composure collapsed. She flew up to her room, slammed the door, and sobbed. Her father, returning from work shortly after Amy arrived, also flew up the stairs, wondering what tragedy had occurred.

"Oh, Amy, it's all right. There'll be other teams. You'll get another chance. Besides, you have so many activities already," he said.

"But, Dad, I'm such a loser. Out of eighteen girls, only three didn't make it."

"There! You see! There are two others who didn't make it either!" Dad was trying to be positive.

"Right! And they're both losers like me! And to think that I talked Jackie into trying out. She made it and I didn't! I'll never try out again—for anything—as long as I live!" Amy cried.

Student Council Elections

The next week, Jason, a freshman at Centerville, stayed up late Monday and Tuesday nights making campaign posters, preparing fliers, and working on his speech. Student Council elections were going to be held Wednesday, and each candidate had to deliver a speech to the student body.

At the end of school on Wednesday, the election results were announced over the public address system just before the final bell: "The new Student Council representatives for grade nine are..." the announcer paused for effect, "Michelle Van Buren and Jeff Pennington. Congratulations to our new representatives, and may they remember their campaign promises, because the rest of us surely will."

"Yeah, we sure will" mumbled several students. "Hey, Jeff, we're counting on that pizza party you promised!" added a classmate.

No one noticed Jason fighting back tears. He slipped quietly out of the classroom as soon as the bell rang and hurried home alone. The next day he refused to go to school, claiming an upset stomach. While Mom and Dad wondered about the sudden illness, they agreed that he could stay home. Dad hung around longer than usual that morning. He seemed to want to say something, but finally he left for work without knowing what he could say to console his son.

Band Tryouts

One day that week Paul, a junior at Centerville, was practicing the trumpet when his mom got home from work. "It sounds good," she said. "I love it when you practice without being told."

Later Paul announced that band tryouts would be held the following week. "Ah! I knew there was a reason for your sudden devotion to practicing," Mom said. "Well, whatever it takes, I'm glad to hear the trumpet."

Paul practiced each night for a week and entered the tryouts confidently. He had been in the concert band for two years, and he hoped to win a spot in the symphonic band. During the audition, Paul played some scales, a piece he had memorized, and a duet with another student.

The next day Mrs. Winter posted the lists of band members. Paul's name was on the list for the concert band. He was disappointed and frustrated. He had not made the symphonic band! He would *not* be in concert band again!

In elementary school and middle school, all instrumentalists are in the band. In high school, membership may be more selective.

To be a sophomore in concert band was all right, but to be a junior in concert band, well... no one did that if they wanted to maintain self-respect.

Feeling Our Children's Pain

As parents we live through the losing times with our children, feeling their pain, wanting to make things better, and offering words of comfort, which often seem to fall on unresponsive ears. We want to fix the situation, making everything all right, just as we did when we placed a Band-Aid on a toddler's scraped knee. But we also know that there's no easy cure for the pain of losing. We grieve with our children. Sometimes we blame the coach, the music director, the judges, the class, or whoever seemed to treat our children unjustly. We side with our children in their battles against unfair competition, unfair selection practices, unfair criteria for entrance. We are sure that they would have made the team if only things had been different. Sometimes our concerns about fair practices are justified, but often we simply need to accept the loss along with our children.

Should schools foster competition among students by sponsoring activities in which there are winners and losers? Should all sports be intramural-type events? Should Student Council members be chosen by teachers, by some objective criteria, or by picking names out of a hat? Is there some way to make all musical groups equal in status?

This is a difficult issue, and one that the Christian school community must face. Inside and outside of the classroom, schools and parents are re-examining the competitive atmosphere our children encounter. Christian educators are being encouraged to use cooperative learning techniques in the classroom, helping students work and learn together, helping each other rather than competing. Some schools, at least through the junior high grades, avoid any selection process and permit everyone to play on the team, participate in band, or sing in choir. Other schools plan only intramural sports programs—anyone in the class can play, and there is no outside competition.

Removing all competition may seem ideal and consistent with the aims of the Christian community, but does it prepare students for the realities of life? Will they not face a selection process for college, for a job, for church office, for community organizations? Or can a non-competitive environment in school help children grow up before they must face the bumps and disappointments of the real world?

How We Can Help

I think that the answer is twofold. First, schools can do some things to minimize the winning-losing situations that occur. Second, we as parents need to help our children deal with defeat, assess our own ego-involvement, and build them up to withstand the trials that life will surely bring their way.

Certainly in the classroom, teachers have an opportunity to use cooperative groups, or learning teams, not exclusively, but for many learning situations. Learning teams are groups of students who each contribute to the group's learning task: reading, gathering material, answering questions, writing group or individual papers with mutual support, studying for a test, or completing a project. The key is that members are dependent on each other to perform part of the task, yet they are individually accountable for the work they do. A cooperative classroom atmosphere can foster a feeling of Christian community in the school. This can soften the competitive aspects of learning and provide a supportive environment in which all students can learn.

Another direction that many schools have taken is to offer such a variety of extracurricular activities that there is literally something for everyone. For example, if you don't make the squad for football cheerleading, you can try out for basketball cheerleading when a new squad is selected.

Many coaches, music and drama directors, club advisors, and other teachers in student leadership positions are very sensitive to student feelings. They deserve commendation for their heroic efforts to ease the disappointment and boost the self-esteem of those not selected for a particular activity. Personal phone calls and private chats have eased the loss for many students. Some teachers write letters to parents suggesting how they can support their children. Many suggest an alternative course of action for a student whose first goal has been thwarted. These efforts are necessary and should occur in all Christian schools where the love of Christ is manifested.

Probably the most important thing for parents NOT to do is to minimize the loss. Naturally, Amy is disappointed that she didn't make the basketball team. It matters very much to her. She may be facing her first real loss in life, and she is grieving. A parent would be wise to feel sad with her rather than coaxing her to feel better.

Diverting children's attention is best done in subtle ways. The parent who says suddenly, 'Well, let's all go out for pizza tonight!" means well, but the offer may be rejected. A better approach might be: "Amy, we haven't had time to plan supper for tonight. It'd be easier if we could eat out. Do you have any suggestions on where we should go?"

Crying with sons and daughters, literally or figuratively, is something all parents should do. Sharing hugs and tears builds a bond that helps family members weather other storms. When teenagers who didn't make the team or win the election are given a hug or shoulder clasp and invited by a parent to talk about it, they are experiencing what a caring family is all about.

Sometimes children are receptive to stories of a parent's experiences in failing to obtain a desired goal. Again, the timing of the sharing is important. I suggest that parents share their own joys and sorrows from their school days whenever a good opportunity arises. Perhaps when Jason announced he was running for Student Council, his parents could share a time they entered a competition and lost. The message is that it's great to enter, they admire someone who tries, they hope he wins, but anytime we run for something we face the possibility of defeat.

Finally, there is the matter of realistic expectations. Perhaps Paul deserved to miss the position in symphonic band because he hadn't practiced diligently until the week before auditions. Sometime after Paul recovers from his initial disappointment, a parent or teacher could help Paul see the role that he played in the event.

How do we know when we don't have what it takes for a sport, an academic task, or an elective office? This is a difficult realization to come to, and parents, in consultation with a coach or teacher, may have to help students realistically face their abilities. We all walk a fine line between encouraging maximum effort, on the one hand, and facing the inevitable, on the other hand.

Turning to God for comfort is the most important source of relief in disappointment. Often we mention this glibly or routinely. But the Christian family that regularly communes with the Lord has a ready source of help that should easily and readily be invoked.

Loss and defeat are part of life. We want to shield our children from such unhappiness. We remember our own defeats, and we hope to spare our children the pain that we endured.

Perhaps we need to concentrate our efforts on helping them deal with the disappointments which will surely come their way, encourage them to assess the situation realistically, and pray that through suffering will come strength to face life's challenges.

New Kids in School: Welcoming the Newcomer

"There is one type of student for whom the new school year may bring more than the normal amount of anticipation and anxiety.... the one whose family has moved into a different community or school district."

For students, the start of a new school year brings with it excitement and anticipation: new teachers, new classmates, new subjects to study, perhaps a new school building, and new social activities.

Most students are eager for the new school year. For some it is a chance to start over, to work harder, to form new friendships, or to get more involved in school activities. For others it is a time to renew friendships, resume former activities, and continue a course of study.

There is one type of student, however, for whom the new school year may bring more than the normal amount of anticipation and anxiety. I am referring to the totally new student, the one whose family has moved into a different community or school district. For this student *everything* is new. This is a student whose life has changed in some profound ways in addition to the school situation.

Let's take the case of a family who has come from out of town. The student is dealing with several significant losses—loss of friends, loss of familiar surroundings, loss of activities, and loss of an established place within the school environment. In addition to feeling the pain of these losses, the student is trying to adjust to new rules, new people, and a new pecking order. The rest of the family is probably unsettled, and family life is probably disrupted because of the move, so the student may not find all the support he or she needs from parents and siblings.

Some families opt to move to a new community during the school year.

The benefits include the fact that kids can become acquainted before summer vacation arrives and can jump right into the new school while activities are in full swing. Other families opt for a summer move because they believe that their children will have an easier time fitting in at the beginning of a new school year. They may also believe that it will be easier for a student to finish a grade in the present school rather than having to catch up in a totally different classroom with a different curriculum.

Our family has made one move during the school year and two moves during summer vacations, and I have concluded that there is no easy answer, nor is there an ideal time for a move. Moving during the school year pushes students into already established school activities, friendship groups, and a certain place in subject areas, all of which can be traumatic and disconcerting. However, it does allow them to establish some connections and associations before summer vacation. Moving during the summer provides a cleaner break between the old and the new, but it can be a long, hot summer for parents: anticipating, moving, and then encouraging an unhappy child while awaiting the start of school.

Helping with the Transition

If your family has moved to a new location, here are some things you as parents can do to help make the transition smoother for your children.

1. *Make it your first priority to help your children become acquainted with the new community and school.* While many things seem to need attention at once—unpacking, redecorating, locating stores, and so on—helping your kids get settled should be at the top of the list.

2. *Visit the school with your children and talk with the principal or counselor.* Even though many schools have an orientation session for new students, getting a personal head start is beneficial.

3. *Find out which students from the school live in your neighborhood and make contact with them or their families.*

4. *Find out which churches many of the students attend and visit them.*

5. *Ask about local youth activities or recreational opportunities:* Little League, soccer, library clubs, play-ground recreation. Encourage your kids to join.

6. *Be willing to have friends over, even if the house is a mess and you're still unpacking.* You may even suggest that each child bring a friend home for pizza on Friday night.

7. *Inquire about other new families in the school.* Make contact with them and get acquainted.

8. *As much as possible, be home for your children when they arrive after school, particularly the first few weeks.* Have a snack at the table, and sit down to chat with them about how things are going

9. *Acknowledge any negative feelings your kids may have about a new school.*

© David Buffington, PhotoDisc

Listen and empathize, but remind your children that it's best not to be too critical at school. Sometimes newcomers chase away possible friends by raving about the old school and criticizing the new.

10. *Keep in touch with the teacher about how the adjustment is going.* Share your own observations and ask how you may help the adjustment process.

Taking Root in the New Community

Parents who have moved have the primary responsibility for helping their children become comfortable in their new surroundings, but families who are already established members of the Christian school community should look for ways to welcome new families. Here are some suggestions for helping transplanted families take root in the new community.

1. *Call the school during the summer and ask for names of new families and their addresses and phone numbers.* If there are many new families, focus on those who have children in the same grades as your children. Perhaps someone would pair each new family with one old family.

2. *Send a note or make a phone call to welcome new families.* Offer to be available for any questions they may have. This gesture can even be directed to their old address if they are arriving late in the summer.

3. *Get together with a new family:* invite the children on an outing with your children, arrange to meet at a local restaurant or have a picnic in the park, invite them to a church service or social event, or offer to accompany them to a school open house or to give them a tour of the school.

4. *Encourage your children to be alert to new students and suggest that they invite them over.*

5. *Have a coffee or dessert time for new parents after the school year has begun.* This can be an informal, get acquainted time in your home, or with other parents at school.

6. *Call the new family once or twice during the first few months of school to express interest in how things are going for them.*

7. *Be available throughout the school year to talk about any concerns that may arise.*

8. *Hold a "Who's New and What's Different?" back-to-school pizza night at school.* The focus can be on new teachers and staff, new students, and new features of the building.

9. *Look for new parents at school functions.* Go out of your way to introduce yourself. Imagine how you would feel awaiting the beginning of a school concert with people all around you chatting and having no one talk to you!

10. *Designate a person or committee from the Parent-Teacher Association to "shepherd" new families through their adjustment period.*

Three Children's Experiences

Our family has moved several times, and our experiences have varied. Here are the stories of how each of our three children encountered a new school.

Caroline was starting the seventh grade, having moved from another state. She had come from a school which she had attended for eight years and where she had many friends. Her first days at the new school were spent eating lunch alone while groups of students ate together, talking and laughing, seemingly oblivious of her. One of the girls was planning a birthday party to which all the other girls had been invited prior to Caroline's arrival. The chatter both in and out of class centered on this upcoming event. Caroline felt lonely, hurt, and very sorry that she had moved.

Were these classmates trying to be cruel? No, I think not. They simply weren't aware of or concerned about how it feels to be new. Perhaps an observant teacher could have intervened, at least to suggest that one or two girls include the new student. Perhaps even a call to the birthday girl's parent would have alerted her to a situation of which she was unaware.

Another time, our son, John, arrived as a new student in a school where everyone knew everyone else. On John's first day in class, the teacher announced, "We have a special honor today. John Post, will you come and stand beside me? John's family moved to our community, and his parents decided to send him to our school because they heard what a good school it is and how friendly we all are. Is that true?"

"Yes," shouted the class.

"I agree," said the teacher. "Now I need one person to be a buddy for the week, to sit next to John, help him find books and papers, and introduce him to the others at recess. Who can be a good buddy?"

Naturally, all hands went up.

One more example deserves mention. Janine arrived in the new city in July, ready to enter her senior year in high school. It was the worst possible time to have to change schools! She spent the summer missing her friends in Cincinnati, especially a boyfriend. She regretted giving up her position as cheerleading captain and the close associations she had through class Bible studies and InterVarsity Christian Fellowship.

Someone in a local church in the new community heard about Janine and called the parents of two girls who would be seniors at the same school. These girls visited Janine. The principal knew of her interest in cheerleading and made sure she knew of the upcoming tryouts. A school parent organized a "New Parents Coffee" soon after the school year began to which we were invited to meet with other new parents.

This was a good start, but even more could have been done. A teacher or counselor could have taken a special interest in Janine during the first few days of school. One or more students could have become buddies to accompany her, or at least check with her during the school day. Finally, some students could have been alerted to the possibility of including her in some Friday night activities.

At school she was pleasant and probably appeared to be fine. But at home each day she cried, wishing someone would ask her to join a weekend event, since she was obviously reluctant to approach groups of students for fear of intruding.

Within our school communities, whether they are Christian or public schools, each of us has an obligation to look out for the welfare of newcomers. Then we will be living up to Jesus' expectations of us, and we truly will be serving him. "I was a stranger and you took me in" (Matthew 25:35b).

The Misfit:
Painful Memories
from Junior High

*"Eighth grade was going to be
the best year of my life. Instead,
it turned out to be the worst."*

It was two months into my eighth grade year. I felt confident. Gone were
the jitters of seventh grade. Gone was some of the baby fat, as my mother
called it, that had plagued me since childhood. "You are developing into
quite a young lady," said the relatives, much to my embarrassment. But it
was unavoidably true.

I had let my hair grow longer, and I could sweep it back in a fashionable
ponytail or let it cascade down my shoulders. Boys looked twice at a girl
with long hair, and other girls envied her. Granted, this was the way it was
in the 50's and 60's, but these kinds of events and emotions are ageless and
exist for current teens as well.

My newly acquired confidence translated into an easy relationship with
my classmates. I made appropriate, clever remarks, and they laughed.
Though I wasn't trying to be the class clown, I was witty, fun, and friendly,
and I enjoyed the attention it brought.

Schoolwork? That was going well, I guess, but it wasn't high on my list of
priorities. I did what was required but saved my greatest energy for social
interactions. I evaluated each class in the school day not by the subject, the
teacher, the location, or the time of day. My sole criterion was who was in the
class. An excellent class had lots of witty, fun, good-looking kids—winners in
the early adolescent popularity contest.

Eighth grade provided lots of social opportunities—games, plays, con-
certs, class picnics, field days, and socializing that went on between classes
and, as much as possible, during classes. There was some rivalry, rather
subtle, concerning who would become the class leaders, and therefore, command the respect and envy of the class. Personality, looks, clothes, and

involvement in athletics were rated, sometimes overtly and sometimes covertly, to see who would make it to the top.

An important component of my new confidence was the arrival of a best friend. I had never really had a best friend before. I always had someone to sit with on the bus, someone else to carpool with to school events, and someone else to have over and to visit in return. But at the beginning of eighth grade, Joan decided that she and I should be best friends. And so we were. We slept over at each other's houses, attended school functions together, hung around together at school, and became known as a twosome.

We spent, or tried to spend, hours on the phone, thwarted only by the two-party telephone system in which each telephone line served two families. Nevertheless, the friendship grew and provided security and stability.

Joan seemed willing to move along in any direction I set. Buoyed by her encouragement and my own rapidly escalating self-confidence, I could tell that eighth grade was going to be a fantastic year!

Confidence Is Threatened

The first blow to my newly acquired confidence was failing to be selected for the cheerleading squad. At least, I told myself, I had made the first cuts. That in itself held some status!

The next blow occurred during auditions for the school play. I didn't even know if I wanted to be in a play, to stand up in front of everyone and recite some silly lines. My voice would probably crack, or I would forget my lines. None of these were important considerations, however, because everyone who was anyone (or at least trying to be) tried out for the play.

I tried out, but it was a disaster. A frog appeared in my

© Ryan McVay, PhotoDisc

throat out of nowhere, and I croaked out my lines, red and embarrassed. Oh well, I told myself, the director would surely be able to see my true potential underneath the jitters. He evidently did see something, because he assigned me the role of a sailor, one of twenty who were to stand in formation on the deck of the H.M.S. *Pinafore!*

Of all the humiliations I could suffer, this one seemed to be the worst. To try out for a leading role, Little Buttercup, and to be awarded the role of a sailor seemed more than I could bear. The other sailors also considered the role beneath their dignity. The way we dealt with our humiliation was by joking with one another about having to wear the silly sailor costumes.

The supreme challenge of that school year arrived the following Monday in the form of a new student. She lived a few blocks from school, and her parents had transferred her to our school because they had just built a house nearby.

One look told me she meant trouble! She was pretty and poised, with just the right mixture of shyness and assertiveness. She dressed well, lived in a nice house, and had an older brother who was an athlete. But her most striking feature was her long, thick, flowing hair—a magnificent mane, "big hair," that was the instant envy of all junior high girls and which, along with her other assets, commanded the attention of the boys. She was a disaster in the making, guaranteed to be a winner in the popularity war.

Soon she had gathered quite a following. The girls were her worshippers; the boys, her admirers. A group of carefully chosen friends became her entourage. But there was also a crowd that hung around the periphery, eager to be included whenever they were permitted to be.

It wasn't long before she announced her first major social undertaking: a sleep-over party to which a large, but select, number of girls would be invited. Her guest list included all of her clique and selected members of the fringe group. Joan and I were in neither.

A girl named Terry from the fringe group was invited. Terry's birthday just happened to be on the day of the great sleep-over, and so the gracious hostess renamed her sleep-over "Terry's Birthday Party." The guest list expanded to include a few of Terry's other friends. My friend Joan was one. I was not.

The situation grew even more complicated. The next momentous discovery was that Joan's birthday was only three days after The Party, an event that was rapidly gaining momentum and social magnitude. The magnanimity of the gracious hostess knew no bounds, it appeared. Her sleep-over event was further renamed "Terry and Joan's Birthday Party." Now a few of Joan's close friends were invited. But somehow I—her best friend—was not.

A party for my own best friend, and I wasn't invited! Could this rival not realize that Joan and I were best friends? That was absurd. Everyone knew it!

I kept up appearances at school. I remained witty, fun, friendly, charming. But at home I was miserable. I cried. I sulked. I thought, "How could anyone do this to me? How could she leave me out of a socially prominent event? And especially one in honor of my best friend!" I was crushed.

Any advice from my parents seemed hollow. "You'll get over it." "These things happen." "That's what growing up is all about."

Who wanted to hear such words? Surely no one had ever been as humiliated and treated as poorly as I had!

Winners and Losers

The party came and went. It was the talk of the school for days before and afterwards. It was the envy of the uninvited, who tried to play it cool with a feigned nonchalance.

While the event itself gradually faded into just another eighth-grade occurrence, the results of the party lingered. They could be seen in many ways. First, the party gave impetus to the beginning of a large, more inclusive crowd that hung around together. Joan became part of it, and her interest in me declined. Second, this new crowd created their own social events and directed class activities. The unofficial popularity contest was over; winners and losers had emerged. Needless to say, I was among the losers.

The school year had started off with such promise. This was to have been my year. Everything was in my favor until it crumbled.

It was a very long school year. Being on the outside was not the way to go through eighth grade. Hearing about others having fun was depressing. My former best friend hardly noticed me anymore, just when I needed her most.

I limped through the school year. Occasional good times were dominated by times of feeling lonely, rejected, and friendless. My rival, besides acquiring social prominence and a large following of friends, became increasingly assertive in putting me down. What began with an obvious but superficial comparison—the two girls with the longest hair in the class—became a power struggle. She giggled to her friends while looking in my direction, ever so subtly, while making sure I caught a glimpse. She played up to Joan, who moved from the outer crowd to the inner clique. She planned events, well within everyone's hearing, and managed to pay just enough attention to the other uninvited class members that they couldn't feel as left out as I felt.

"I like your blouse. Wherever did you get it? I've been looking all over for one like that!" she said to a classmate who was considered to be rather plain, and the girl went away glowing.

"Ted, you are so-o-o good at math, and I just can't do it at all. Will you help me?" These words were given full effect with a dazzling smile, a flick of the hair off the shoulders, and the batting of eyelashes. It worked like a charm. The world was at her fingertips.

"Oh, Arden," she said one day. "I've been meaning to talk to you. I heard that you felt left out when I had that sleep-over a while ago. It just sort of happened that it ended up being for Terry and Joan. I never intended to have a party for your best friend and not invite you."

I forced myself to answer, "That's okay; I was busy anyway. I hope you had a good time!"

That was all she needed. She began an exciting tale of the wonderful party: who had attended, what they had done, and on and on. I fought back tears, smiled sweetly, and excused myself to the restroom, where I burst into tears.

The school year drew to the end even though I thought it never would. Over the summer I developed a friendship with a new neighbor who had recently arrived from a foreign country with her family, and she became my new best friend. Although we never attended the same school, she sustained me through high school.

My rival and her crowd dominated the ninth grade year at high school as they had eighth grade. She remembered to send little jabs my way. She retained the admiration of most of the class and scored some real coups by winning a spot on the cheerleading squad and dating senior boys.

Unfortunately, my experience of feeling left out isn't unusual. Many of us who have weathered the storms of youth can reminisce with honesty about similar feelings of loneliness or even ostracism.

In junior high I never did reach the stage where I could say with the Apostle Paul, "I have learned the secret of being content in any and every situation. . . . " (Philippians 4:12b). I doubt that many teens, especially early teens, do reach that point. It isn't until much later that we see how our early, painful experiences have been used by God to mold us according to his will and purpose for our lives.

Some Lessons Well Learned

My teen experiences made me a different person than I would have been had my dreams of social prominence come true. The lessons I learned are similar to what others tell me they learned through similar experiences. Those of us who survived junior high have adopted the following goals:

- To never intentionally disregard another person's feelings.
- To become loving and caring to a wide range of fellow human beings.
- To ache with those who ache and feel a real empathy with the rejected.
- To look beyond what society sees, and to look into the heart.
- To recognize all human beings as created in the image of God, equal in his eyes, and called upon to serve him and others.
- To serve God above all, and to love our neighbor as our self.

Could these lessons be just the result of growing up and looking at the world as an adult? I don't think so. The influence of early experiences is indelibly etched on each of our lives. We remember social and emotional pain from our early years, and this pain helps shape the adults that we become. I hope that we, young and old, can turn these experiences to our profit and to the profit of others.

Advice to Parents

If you have teens going through some tough social times at school, there are a few things you can do:

First, give them all the love, support, and encouragement you can. Listen to them and encourage them to share. Empathize without always trying to suggest solutions.

Second, consider talking to a teacher or the principal if the situation seems prolonged and is causing great distress. School personnel may have some insight into the situation and will surely want to know about it.

Third, you may want to consider a new school, at least on a trial basis. This step should be taken only if all other measures fail.

Fourth, assure your kids that nothing lasts forever, except the love of God. This may be a time to draw closer to him to experience the comfort and love he promises in times of need.

Healing the Hurt:
Teaching Kindness and Respect

"Some students had been ostracized by fellow students, while others had been overtly or covertly harassed by cruel words or actions."

"I can't believe it!" snapped Ms. Turner, as she left the faculty meeting. "Are they trying to make us responsible for the *social* lives of students, too? As if we don't have enough to do! They expect us to try all of these educational innovations—literature-based reading, balanced literacy, skills instruction, critical thinking, cooperative learning, brain-based learning—and now we're supposed to make our school a caring Christian community. I remember the days when a teacher's job was to *teach!*"

Mr. Swenson, a second-year teacher who rarely spoke up, felt the blush creeping up his neck as his anger rose. "But that's part of teaching! We're concerned about every aspect of our students' lives, and their social interactions are a very important part of their lives. Isn't this part of training a child 'in the way of the Lord'?"

Ms. Turner looked stunned. She opened her mouth, let out a loud "Humph!" and hurried away, muttering something about young teachers and new ideas.

Ms. Turner and Mr. Swenson had just participated in a faculty discussion concerning what the school should do about recent instances of social ostracism and harassment. The principal chose her words deliberately. Some students had been ostracized by fellow students, while others had been overtly or covertly harassed by cruel words or actions.

The impetus for the discussion came from several parents who had shared upsetting stories with the principal. One father said that his daughter received phone calls that included derogatory comments about her looks, clothes, and personality. While the caller never identified herself, his daughter thought it was a schoolmate. Another parent announced that his daughter

The children's book, Swimmy, *by Leo Lionni, inspired an art project and bulletin board emphasising a cooperative learning environment.*

would not be returning to the Christian school in the fall because she felt excluded and had no friends, citing examples of students making fun of her. Still another parent worried about the popularity accorded to athletes. Her son said he was tired of being called a nerd just because he was small, studious, and unathletic. All of the parents wanted to know what the school was doing about such problems.

The principal told each parent that she would look into the school's policy on such matters and discuss it with the teachers. Even as she agreed to do this, she wondered if social issues were, in fact, the school's responsibility.

Left Out

"Did you hear about Sara Lickert's birthday party?" Cheryl Jones asked Susan Sanderson. "It's the annual event that leaves my Jenny in tears—a week before and a week after. She's never been invited, but it seems that all the other girls in the class are! All they talk about is what they'll do at the party and what presents to buy—as if Sara needs presents! I wish the Lickerts would use their money to do something for the whole class, or at least all of the girls!"

"Yes, I heard about the party. My daughter Jill was invited. She wants to go, of course, and I suppose I'll let her. But I am concerned about the hard feelings Sara's parties cause. Each year it seems that every girl hopes she isn't left out. It happened to Jill once, so I know how Jenny feels. Why do the Lickerts let Sara exclude just a few?"

"I wish the teachers would do something. After all, they must see what's going on!" exclaimed Cheryl.

"Last year Jill's teacher sent home a note about parties," Susan replied.

"He asked parents to send invitations in the mail. He also asked that they invite 'all or just a few'—those were his words. Some parents were angry. They said it was none of his business."

"Well, I think it is the school's business! That's where the kids are all together. That's what schools are for—to teach kids how to get along, to respect each other, to develop responsibility for each other. They talk a lot about cooperative learning; this group business is supposed to get them to be responsible for each other's learning. How about getting them to be responsible for each other's feelings? Christian schools, especially, should teach kindness and consideration!" Cheryl retorted.

The School's Problem

Christian schools have often been expected to be more than the local public schools—more in terms of teacher commitment, more in terms of a carefully planned curriculum that recognizes God's authority in the universe, more in terms of caring for students.

Today Christian schools are called upon to assume responsibility for more and more aspects of their students' lives, as are public schools. They find themselves assisting children of divorce, accommodating children of working parents, helping students plan for and carry out homework assignments, and encouraging parent involvement in their children's education. Lately some Christian schools have been asked by parents to get involved in students' social interactions. These schools are asking themselves the following questions:

- What can the school do about students' social events outside of school? Should it interfere? If so, when and how?
- How much should the school monitor students' talk and social behavior within the school setting? Are teachers responsible for stopping unkind comments? Should the school limit itself to severe cases of ostracism or harassment brought to its attention by parents?
- At what grade level, if any, does the school take a hands-off policy? While most schools have policies of expected student behavior and some include statements about respect for others, few have addressed the school's role in social matters. The school is asked to intervene when a parent becomes aware that an extremely upset son or daughter has experienced repeated taunts, frequent harassment, or continual rejection. The parent calls the school, demanding to know what will be done.

Some Solutions

One midwestern Christian school addressed these issues by calling a parent-teacher meeting. A series of incidents that had been related to the principal were shared with the group. Parents raised additional concerns, and a panel of parents and teachers discussed them. A guest speaker provided some thoughts and ideas. Small group discussions were arranged to identify areas for further study and proposed action. Easy and quick solutions didn't result, but the group realized that they had a common concern and committed themselves to finding solutions.

The following suggestions may help the Christian school community talk about ways to create a climate for responsible Christian social behavior.

1. Devotions and Discussion

A series of devotionals on the theme of social interactions could be used concurrently in school and at home. The school would inform parents of the theme and the biblical passages, and parents could discuss them with their children. One young man told me that when his class was studying the fruits of the Spirit (Galatians 5:22-23), everyone was kinder to each other. Schools could emphasize one spiritual fruit per month and study related Scripture passages, informing parents of planned weekly devotions. Studying the Beatitudes is a popular school theme, too, because it focuses our attention on the qualities God blesses.

Studying the Beatitudes reminds us all of the characteristics Jesus values.

2. Prayer

Personal prayer for each other in the Christian community should be a part of our lives. Prayer within school settings could focus on social needs as well as the physical and intellectual needs we typically include. I wonder what would happen if each of us—parents, teachers, and students—prayed daily to be more Christ-like in our words and deeds?

3. Alertness and Awareness

Just as parents need to be aware of what their children are doing and saying, teachers need to be alert to what occurs in the classroom, hallways, and school grounds as much as possible. Teachers' schedules and duties do not permit them to eavesdrop on all student conversations, nor should they. However, it is appropriate for teachers to confront a student on the spot or at a later time and to question behavior suspected to be cruel or hurtful. A series of incidents or serious problems could then be discussed at a faculty meeting.

4. Confrontation and Counseling

Sometimes a teacher overhears conversations suggesting harassment or exclusion. Such instances may warrant counseling in addition to confrontation. For example, one teacher overheard some students calling a foreign-born student a derogatory name. The teacher calmly asked the offending students to see him during lunch hour. He asked them why they were doing this and to imagine how they would feel if someone called them names. After a brief discussion, he suggested that they apologize to the student they offended and then sent them on their way. He kept an eye on the situation and discussed it at the next faculty meeting.

5. Community

As part of a Christian community, we are one in Christ. Not only should our unity enable us to work together, it should compel us to be responsible for and to each other. This means that I must care when your child is hurting or left out, and I must do something about it. I may need to speak to you or your child. Likewise, you must care about my child. We both need to be open to hearing about something hurtful our children may have done.

6. Communication

A Christian community that shares the love of Christ and works together for Christian education must keep the lines of communication open. Parents and school personnel must share not only news of school events, conferences, and student progress, but also areas of concern.

Giving and Receiving

Parents in the Christian school community should be willing to give and receive help when it appears that a few students are being excluded from activities. One parent discovered that her daughter hadn't invited two girls from her class to a birthday party she was planning. The mother found out about it when another mom, whose daughter had been invited, mentioned the fact. The girl who was planning the party was given an ultimatum by her mother: invite all the girls or cancel the party.

Likewise, we need to be open to teachers who give us information about more than our children's academic progress. They help us understand how our children interact with peers in the school setting. We need to receive this information in Christian love, avoid becoming defensive, and deal with problems.

Public schools face similar issues, and faculty and staff may have discussions similar to those cited here. This article is not meant to suggest that only Christian schools should address social problems or that public schools don't do so. Certainly public schools are as committed to fostering peaceful and harmonious student interaction. Administrators, teachers, and parent in every community have the same aims. However, it would seem that schools that bear the name of Christ have a covenantal mandate to address these issues.

Many schools hold several parent-teacher meetings each year. The importance of parents and teachers getting together regularly cannot be overestimated. Such meetings are valuable in raising issues, addressing concerns, and setting agendas for action.

In response to Ms. Turner's question about whether or not the school is responsible for creating a caring community, we must answer with a resounding, "Yes!" But we must add that it takes parents and schools working together to achieve it.

Facilitating
Literacy
and Learning
at Home

Boosting
Reading at Home

*"Reading side by side as parent and child is a special time
of togetherness, providing one way for parents to foster a
love of reading and a curiosity about the printed word."*

A conscientious father, an avid reader himself, was reading to his kindergarten daughter one night. The girl was totally absorbed in both the story
and the illustrations. She frequently interrupted her father: "Daddy, what's
that? Is that the 'woof'? What's he doing? Where's Red Riding Hood?" Her
questions seemed to flow endlessly.

"Now just listen to the story and you'll find out," was his somewhat
exasperated reply. "If you keep interrupting, we'll never finish the story!"
Although this dad probably had the best of intentions, he apparently failed
to consider some of the reasons he and his daughter engaged in this nightly
activity.

Reading side by side as parent and child is a special time of togetherness,
providing one way for parents to foster a love of reading and a curiosity
about the printed word. Most teachers and reading experts agree that reading with a child is the best way to encourage a positive attitude toward
reading. Reading to infants and preschoolers facilitates their literacy development. As the child approaches kindergarten, a parent can stop occasionally to let the youngster guess the next word or figure out the next event.
The parent should encourage questions and talk about the story. In this
way, the child can become a participant in the reading process, rather than
merely an observer.

Creating a Reading Environment

Here are eleven other suggestions for ways to stimulate reading in your
home and foster a positive reading atmosphere in your family.

1. *Visit the library.* The librarian can help family members of all ages find

John Post reads a "board" book to Simon, age 1. Board books enable even young children to handle books.

books of interest at an appropriate level of difficulty. Many libraries sponsor story groups or reading clubs which children can join.

2. *Leave written messages for your children.* For children who are just beginning to read, you might want to try writing messages in the form of rebuses, a combination of words and pictures.

3. *Read together as a family.* Family devotions, with a variety of Bibles, Bible storybooks, and study books, can provide a perfect opportunity for family reading.

4. *Read everything in sight.* Read with your children the words on cereal boxes, food wrappers, directions for games, street signs, billboards, and elsewhere. Words are everywhere! One game you can play in the car requires children to systematically find a word beginning with each letter of the alphabet on road signs and billboards.

5. *Have a variety of reading materials around the house.* Magazines, newspapers, joke or riddle books, encyclopedias, atlases, and "how-to" books are just a few examples. You should also be willing to tolerate good comic books because they provide fun reading and can inspire the reluctant reader.

6. *Provide books of different reading levels from "easy" to "hard."* Children can become discouraged and uninterested if everything they find to read around the house requires a great deal of effort.

7. *Provide many different kinds of books.* Not every reader has the same tastes, so tempt youngsters with different sorts of literature: fantasy, science

fiction, historical fiction and biographies, contemporary realistic fiction, information books, and poetry. Garage sales are good sources of inexpensive reading materials.

8. *Recognize your children's special interests.* Subscribe to magazines that interest your child or relate to one of his or her hobbies. Encourage your youngster to do "research" on a favorite sport or a special hobby.

9. *Share reading materials of interest.* Clip a newspaper article on fishing for the fishing enthusiast. Post a newspaper cartoon on the refrigerator when it exemplifies a humorous family occurrence.

10. *Leave reading material where it is enticing.* If you do the "library shopping" for the whole family, spread out the new treasures on the floor or table where attention can be drawn to them rather than stacking the new reading material neatly on the book shelf.

Now that he's 2 years old, Simon eagerly "reads" a book by himself.

11. *Finally, be a reader yourself.* Children often follow the example set by their parents. They will notice the importance you attach to reading for information and the joy you derive from reading for pleasure.

The International Reading Association offers several free booklets for parents to assist children's reading and writing development. (See order form on pp. 191-192). States have reading organizations that also provide helpful publications at a nominal charge. (See reference to the Michigan Reading Association on p. 188).

Reading is a lifelong skill that is necessary for contemporary life and that provides a source of pleasure. Early habits and attitudes can last a lifetime. A good start and proper encouragement contribute to the formation of an avid adult reader.

Parents Pledge to Help

The importance of parents in fostering a child's reading is immeasurable. The Parent Committee of the Michigan Reading Association suggested several commitments that parents should make to help their children become readers. Adaptations of these suggestions follow:

I will help my child start a word collection, using cards to place on the refrigerator or in a recipe box. We will read them over often.

I, or someone else, will read with my child daily. I will not force my child to read aloud to me but will alternate reading aloud with my child. I may even do all or most of the reading if he or she balks at reading aloud.

I, or someone else, will take dictation (talk written down) of a story or poem my child may want to create, and I will help him/her to read their own words.

I will help my child pursue a topic or author of interest and find books to read by visiting the local library, school library, or bookstore with my child. I will display these books at home, rather than just setting them on a shelf, to entice my child to read.

I will praise my child for at least one success daily.

I will help my child find others with whom to read: another child, sibling, grandparent or a friend.

I will allow my child to buy books and educational games, and we will limit the amount of TV viewing my child does.

I will talk to my child daily about school and reading and show enthusiasm for what they read and learn.

I will assist my child in using the Internet wisely and find sites that support literacy.

I will obtain some CD-Roms like the Talking Storybooks and the Jump Start Series for young children and adventures that teach content areas like Carmen Sandiego and The Oregon Trail for older children.

Book displays — in the library, in school, and at home — entice young readers.

A Reading Program That Works: Sustained Silent Reading (SSR)

*"Children improve their
reading ability by reading a lot."
"Independent reading increases both
vocabulary and reading fluency."*

I'll never forget the morning I walked into a school and cheerily greeted the secretary, only to be hushed into silence in a manner that suggested I'd better heed her warning. After seeing the puzzled look on my face, she ushered me into an adjoining office and proceeded to tell me what was going on.

The school was having USSR, she explained, and everyone, yes, everyone was to observe it. Still not comprehending, I searched my memory for a school bulletin that informed us of the arrival of Russian visitors, but not recalling any, I asked what Russian observance was occurring. She laughed and told me that this had nothing to do with the former Soviet Union. USSR stood for Uninterrupted Sustained Silent Reading, a new program the school had begun. Recently, it is simply referred to as SSR.

SSR operates on the principle that students need time to read—independently and silently—materials of their choice, other than the reading required for classwork. The school which I visited was observing an important component of this program—everyone reads: the students, the teacher, the principal, the secretary, the janitor. This school literally had everyone reading. All classes and all persons were involved.

Sustained Silent Reading

Typically, a program is set up in the following way.

First, a time is set up for SSR such as 8:30-9:00. Frequently, elementary schools have varying amounts of time, depending on the grade. First graders may spend 5-10 minutes on SSR, and sixth graders may spend 30 minutes. Often teachers begin the year with a small amount of time and increase it gradually.

Second, materials are provided from which students may choose what they want to read. Often, the students have obtained books from home or the library. However, the classroom may also contain a variety of reading material such as magazines, books, almanacs, encyclopedias, and newspapers. Depending on the school and the students, comic books, food wrappers, and other unusual reading material may also be available. While some may frown at the thought of dignifying this sort of reading material, some unorthodox materials may inspire reluctant or remedial readers to read.

Third, agreement is reached that everyone who is in the program will read. If the program is confined to a classroom, the teacher and students agree to read. Enlisting the principal's participation is a real incentive, especially if the principal visits a different class each day to do his or her reading. No one is permitted to do homework, to make up tests, or to use the time in any other way. This includes the teacher! Everyone's involvement in reading demonstrates the importance of taking time to read.

Fourth, the three words are taken seriously. *Sustained* means we read for the entire time allotted. *Silent* means that we are as quiet as possible and that we read silently. *Reading* means that we get together with a good book (or other reading material) and READ, READ, READ!

Some parents, when first informed about a program such as SSR, ask why the teacher is taking time for students to read silently. Shouldn't the teacher be instructing students? Isn't that what school is for?

Of course, a good teacher engages in much direct instruction. However, some interesting research in the field of reading points to independent reading as a very important and profitable use of time. Consider the following

A school poster promotes reading books instead of watching TV.

claims made in a report by the U.S. Department of Education: "Children improve their reading ability by reading a lot. Reading achievement is directly related to the amount of reading children do in school and outside. Independent reading increases both vocabulary and reading fluency. Research shows that the amount of leisure time spent reading is directly related to children's reading comprehension, the size of their vocabularies, and their gains in their reading ability" (U.S. Dept. of Education, 1986, p. 11). Research has constantly supported and reaffirmed these findings (Post, 2000; Vacca et al., 2000).

This report supports numerous other research studies and informal observations that suggest the value of time spent simply reading. While many parents would agree with encouraging children to read on their own, some would still question the use of class time for this activity. But the same Education Department report contends: "Unlike using workbooks and performing computer drills, reading books gives children practice in the 'whole act' of reading, that is both in discovering the meanings of individual words and in grasping the meaning of an entire story" (p. 11).

Recent trends in the teaching of reading lead us away from spending large amounts of time on isolated drills such as phonics, and spending more time in the actual reading of books. This is not to say that we omit teaching the letter-sound correspondence. But as children learn a particular sound, such as the short *a* in *hat*, they should spend time reading books with that sound, like *The Cat in the Hat* by Dr. Seuss, instead of doing several worksheets, workbook pages, or drills on the chalkboard or computer. SSR provides just such a time, free from pressure, free for enjoyment. The teacher may even refer to some of the materials which the children have read during SSR at a later time for instructional or review purposes.

A number of schools across the country now use SSR or one of its relatives: DEAR: Drop Everything and Read; SQuiRT: Sustained Quiet Reading Time or SQUiRT: Sustained Quiet Uninterrupted Reading Time; T-20: Take 20 (minutes); WEB: Wonderfully Exciting Books (Routman, 1991); RABBIT: Read A Book Because It's Terrific (Farris, 2000). Reports from teachers and principal are enthusiastic. One teacher notes that her class actually loves to read now, whereas they used to groan at the mention of reading time.

Parents Commit to SSR

How does SSR affect parents? In two ways, I believe. First, ask your children's teachers and the principal if such a program is under consideration at your school.

Second, try to set up a similar program at home. What a great way to extend the benefits of SSR beyond the school! Here's how:

1. *Get a commitment from some or all family members to participate.* Obvi-

ously, if a teenager has sports practice and then work after school, he or she may not be able to take part.

2. *Agree on a time, perhaps 15 minutes after supper each evening.* You may need to specify certain days when SSR can fit your schedule.

3. *Have plenty of appealing reading material around:* books from the public or school library, magazines, an encyclopedia, an almanac, a dictionary, and any other materials which might inspire children to read, such as directions to games, travel brochures, comic or joke books, atlases, city or state maps, a cereal box, a booklet on how to care for pets, or recipes for favorite foods.

4. *Locate a quiet place where you will not be disturbed.* Let all others know that interruptions are only to occur in the case of an emergency.

5. *Put the plan into action for a week and then evaluate it.* Changes can be made at that point. Find something workable for your family.

6. *Spend a few minutes after the SSR time to share something from your reading.* Children love to share and to have an audience. You can show your enthusiasm for reading by sharing what you have read, too.

Micah Anderle shares a book with his family. His supper includes two vegetables he read about in the book: beets and corn.

Seeing parents spend time reading and being excited about it tells children that reading is an important, enjoyable, worthwhile activity!

Benefits of SSR

According to Vacca et al. (1987, 2000), there are several positive messages about reading that children learn by participating in SSR at school or at home.

1. *Reading books is important.* Children develop a sense of what teachers and parents value. Children who spend most of their class time or homework time on hand-outs will regard completing "work" as important. Children who get to read will perceive reading as important

2. *Reading is something anyone can do.* Even young children can "read" by paging through a book. Disabled readers have the chance to read something of their choice without fear of errors or correction.

3. *Reading is communicating with an author.* Children get to respond to an author's message and share that response with others. This is the essence of reading: interaction between author and reader. Reading orally in groups or completing worksheets involves responding primarily to the teacher.

4. *Children are capable of staying on task.* Often children have difficulty paying attention or staying on task for sustained periods of time. SSR has been found to keep children's attention for long periods. They actually look forward to its peacefulness and become absorbed in their books.

5. *Books are meant to be read in large sections.* Basal reading books, or anthologies, contain short excerpts of stories. By reading books, children learn about whole stories and extended pages of print.

6. *Comprehension is the focus of reading,* and SSR will help children focus on comprehension. By reading for a period of time without corrections and questions from a teacher or parent, the child is likely to focus on what the material is saying instead of focusing on oral reading or answers to questions. While parents and teachers should not turn the time following SSR into a question and answer session, sharing something about the book or telling how the book made one feel can aid comprehension. In order to share something about the book, the child needs to comprehend.

7. *Children's judgment is respected in what they read.* Independence is encouraged in choosing reading material, although teacher and parents may offer advice. Children need to develop some responsibility for their own learning. They also have a desire to be in control of some facets of their lives. Choosing what they will read independently fosters this in a positive way.

I hope you'll give it a try. You may find that your children respond like the young child who said, "Is SSR time up already? Let's keep on reading!" or another child who said, "Hurry up, Mom and Dad, it's time to read." That suggests a good title for our reading-at-home program-H.U.R.a.H.: Hurry Up-Read at Home.

Reading Aloud
With Your Kids

"Dad is determined to follow the teacher's suggestion. He opens up to the first page and asks Chris to read. 'No, Dad, you read!' replies Chris."

Just because your kids are old enough to read on their own doesn't mean that you should stop reading aloud to them and with them.

Seven-year-old Christopher is slowly developing the sound-symbol connection, and his teacher has suggested that he practice his reading at home 15 minutes each night. Chris has brought a book home from school, and Dad is determined to follow the teacher's suggestion. He opens up to the first page and asks Chris to read.

"No, Dad, you read!" replies Chris.

Dad reads two pages and says, hopefully, "Okay your turn!" Chris begins to read. He gets stuck on several words, so Dad helps him sound them out—some successfully and others not.

"You read now, Dad!" exclaims Chris.

"But you didn't finish the page!" says Dad.

"I'm sick of sounding out words! Let's just forget it!" Chris is clearly frustrated, as is his dad.

Assess the Home Reading Atmosphere

Fortunately, Chris' dad decided to "let it go" and did some thinking about the home reading atmosphere. When parents encounter reluctant readers like Chris, they should evaluate what's going on. Here are some aspects to examine:

Interest. Ask if your child is interested in the book. A child who is interested in the topic of sports, for example, might be turned off by biography, unless it's about a famous athlete.

Familiarity. Many parents remember reading the same books over and over

74

Janine and Micah Anderle read aloud together each night before bed.

again with the children because kids like things that are familiar. However, other books in the same series or by the same author provide an opportunity to expand beyond one or two favorites. Marc Brown's Arthur books, Joanna Cole's Magic School Bus series, and Paulette Bourgeois's Franklin series are especially popular with young readers. Other series that remain well liked are the Curious George books by H. A. and Margret Rey, the Madeline books by Ludwig Bemelmans, and the Clifford Books by Norman Bridwell.

Level of reading material. Sometimes a child's reading ability doesn't match the level of the book a parent is trying to use. This was a problem for Chris and his father. Picking an easier book could turn their experience into a pleasant interaction rather than a struggle.

Timing. Sometimes parents find themselves reading with their child just before bedtime, when both parent and child are tired and frazzled. Arranging for a more pleasant reading time, such as right after supper, could alleviate this problem.

Sounding it out. A further complication occurs when parents try to help the beginning reader pronounce a word by telling the child to sound it out. The child haltingly tries each syllable in the word but may not succeed in putting all the sounds together. If not, the parent may provide the word. This isn't a bad strategy, but it shouldn't occur more than two or three times per page of twenty to thirty words. A good maxim is, "Provide help and move on!"

Share Reading Between Parent and Child

When parent and child establish a shared reading format, their literacy interaction becomes more positive. Many young readers stumble when they're asked to read a whole story or even a whole page. And good readers who sail along easily can get so caught up in sounding good that they fail to understand the text. But turning reading into a joint venture encourages comprehension and makes the process more enjoyable. The child may read fewer words in a shared reading situation, but the young reader will be developing confidence while receiving the parent's support.

1. *Echo reading*, in which the child reads aloud following the parent's reading of a sentence or partial sentence, helps the child to read independently while imitating fluent oral reading. Even preschoolers may want to

Eight Read Aloud Strategies

1. Echo reading. You read a line or portion of dialog, and your child repeats it, imitating your expression.
2. Choral reading. You and your child read a passage aloud together.
3. Repeated reading. Your child reads a small section two or three times orally to improve fluency and expression.
4. Dialog reading. Both you and your child take the parts of characters, and you also assume the role of narrator.
5. Alternate sentence or paragraph reading. Similar to dialog reading, you take turns reading each sentence or each paragraph.
6. Reading silently. Both you and your child read a section silently. Either of you may then read it aloud before you talk about it.
7. Favorite-part reading. You and your child each read a favorite part of a story that you have practiced either orally or silently.
8. Reading to verify. Either you or your child searches for a section to read aloud that supports something you have said about the story.

"read" a few words after mom or dad does.

2. *Choral reading* is a popular activity in which parent and child read aloud together. The parent may take the lead, with the child reading a second or two behind the parent.

3. *Repeated reading* of a passage also produces greater fluency. Allowing children to tape-record their reading, listen to it, and reread the passage while recording it again may encourage young readers, who can hear their improvement with each repetition.

4. *Dialog reading* is another effective strategy. Each reader assumes the part of one of the characters in the story. The parent may assume the roles of several characters, while the child reads a smaller amount of text. (For a book without dialog, alternating the reading of sentences or paragraphs achieves similar results.)

5. When a parent and child *alternate reading* sentences or paragraphs, children become immersed in turn-taking. This approach also seems to make oral reading fun instead of the laborious reading of the whole page.

6. *Reading silently* becomes more common as students advance in school, so it is good for your child to practice this at home. This gives him or her a chance to work out the kinks before reading aloud. The parent should invite the child to ask about any words he or she wants help with. Parent and child should then talk about what is happening in the book.

7. *Favorite-part reading* is a way for both parent and child to select a short section of the chapter or story to read orally.

8. *Reading to verify* is a good way to promote comprehension and critical thinking as children progress in their reading ability. Either the child or parent asks a question. Then the other person must find and read aloud a part of the text that supports the answer.

Enjoy the Oral Reading Experience

Chris and his dad tried some of these suggestions and turned their reading time into an enjoyable experience. Let's visit a new scene with Chris and his dad. Chris has brought home a book from the Frog and Toad series by Arnold Lobel.

"Which chapter would you like to read?" asks Dad.

"You mean I don't have to read the whole book?" questions Chris.

"Well, let's start with a chapter and then decide," Dad replies.

"Here, you read the first page," Chris suggests.

Dad reads, hanging back a little and hoping that Chris will join in. He does, often supplying words when Dad pauses.

"Let's read aloud together. You seem to know this well," Dad proposes in a low-key way.

"Okay, just for a few pages. Then let's take parts like we did in school. We

Tanner Cone "reads" his favorite book about bears to his father, Mitch.

had a group read Toad's parts, a group read Frog's parts, and a group read the narrator's parts. Know what a narrator is?" Chris was getting excited.

"Tell me," says Dad.

Soon they decide that Dad will be Frog because he is bigger, and Chris will be Toad. When Chris comes to a word he doesn't know, Dad encourages him to sound it out. After a few words, Chris says, "That's enough sounding out. Let's just read!" Dad then supplies the pronunciation for words Chris doesn't know, keeping a mental note of the words so they can return to them at another time.

This evening will be repeated many times in the future as Dad adjusts to Chris' interests, reading level, familiarity, comfort in oral reading, and ability to sound out words. They'll use a combination of choral reading, repeated reading, and dialogue reading. Dad allows Chris to take the lead, and he runs with it.

Interacting over books by sharing the reading and then talking about it can enhance a child's enjoyment, confidence, and skill in reading. The bond between you and your children is strengthened when you read together. And the benefits will continue, because when your children grow up and have kids of their own, they will pattern their reading times on the memories they have of reading at home with you.

Note: I wrote an article for the Grand Rapids Children's Museum outlining ways to interact with children through oral reading of Dr. Seuss books. A copy can be obtained by e-mailing your name and address to <u>apost@calvin.edu</u>. I can also be contacted through the Education Department at Calvin College.

The Lifetime Reader *by Arden Ruth Post*

Mom (Dad) read to me when I was young
And it was always lots of fun.
(S)he gave me time to look and say
Words and questions along the way.

And when I entered seventh grade
(S)he didn't figure I had it made.
But bought and borrowed books galore.
And those I just could not ignore — because
   (S)he spread them on the floor.

And when high school years hit
I had a book (s)he didn't like one bit.
"Why are you reading that?" (s)he asked.
She showed concern, which was not masked.

"It's just what all the kids are reading,"
I said and knew where (s)he was leading.
It wasn't what (s)he would approve.
Would (s)he ask me to remove — it?

No, (s)he didn't ask me not to read it.
Instead, she said, "Well, may I see it?
I'd like to read it, too, you see.
What interests you will interest me."

Reluctantly, I gave it to her (him)
She read the book from cover to cover
"That's really quite a book you've got,"
(S)he said, as in my stomach there formed a knot!

"Tell me what you think about it."
And so we started to discuss it.
And that's the way it was with me.
To *read, read, read* — Mom (Dad) inspired me.

Now that I am fully grown
And I have some children of my own.
We read and read and read some more
And reading never is a chore.

Because we choose books that are fun
Or books of interest to everyone.
Wait — I hear someone knocking at my door —
It just might be the neighbor (or kids) next door.

(S)he really isn't such a bore
But I have something I'd rather do more
Something I've been doing before
I'd just rather read some more.

Parents & Schools:
The Home–School Relationship

"Parents ask, 'Just what role do I play in my child's education? What does the teacher expect of me? How much involvement should I have in the school?'"

"Everyone Gains in Home-School Collaborations" could be the title of many articles and talks as educators seek to enlist parents' assistance in their children's education. The statement reflects a popular theme in education today—that a high level of parental involvement leads to better schools and better learning.

Christian schools have generally tended to foster a high rate of parental involvement and a considerable amount of parent-teacher interaction. Parental ownership in the educational process is often attributed to the biblical mandate which Christian parents embrace: "Train a child in the way he should go, and when he is old he will not turn from it" (Proverbs 22:6). Christian parents take this command seriously and assign the major portion of a child's academic training to the Christian school while assuming a supportive role. Parents do not abdicate responsibility for teaching their children but enter into a partnership with the Christian school in the educational task.

Christian parents may also be committed to public schools for a number of reasons. They believe children's religious beliefs are developed and sustained at home and in the church. Their children will be witnesses in the world and learn to interact with a variety of people. These parents are as interested in fostering positive relationships with their neighborhood schools as are parents in Christian schools.

While a close relationship between home and school is readily acknowledged as beneficial to a child's learning, questions often arise about specifics. Parents ask, "Just what role do I play in my child's education? What does the teacher expect of me? How much involvement should I have in the school?"

After twenty-five years in the field of education—as a teacher, a parent, and most recently an instructor of future teachers—I'd like to share some

A wall display in the Cambridge Christian School in Ontario, Canada, captures the parent-school connection.

observations on strengthening the bond between home and school. Let's begin by considering five of the most common opportunities for parent-school connections.

Open House

Most schools hold an open house or a back-to-school night for parents at the beginning of the school year. At the elementary school level this event consists of a meeting with the child's teacher in the classroom to give parents a general overview of the school year, the curriculum, field trips, the teacher's policies, and any other information the teacher feels will be helpful. At the middle and secondary levels, the open house often involves going through a condensed schedule of the student's day.

It is advisable to attend these events in order to learn about the coming year, to show support for the teacher, and to gain a glimpse of your child's school world for the next nine months. There may be opportunities to volunteer for class outings or projects. Furthermore, attendance at the open house reflects your interest in your child's education.

One word of caution: open house is not the time to engage a teacher in an extended conversation about specific needs or concerns. Such conversations should be scheduled for another time. Many teachers have endured one parent's monologue while longingly watching other parents leave without having a chance to meet them.

Parent-Teacher Conferences

Schools typically schedule parent-teacher conferences or interviews in the fall and again in the winter or spring. Both parents should attend parent-teacher conferences if possible. You will gain information about how your child is doing in specific subject areas, his or her social interactions, behavior, study habits, and skills. Teachers will benefit from information you provide about the student or family which may reflect upon classroom performance.

Parent-teacher conferences are invaluable! Most parents come away with renewed support for the school along with gaining awareness of their kids. You will certainly be able to use the conference as a springboard for conversation at home:

"I hear that you'll be visiting the courthouse next week!"

"Mr. V. was impressed with your project!"

"Mrs. B. suggested you do well on math problems when you slow down and check your answers."

"Ms. P. asked us to help you set up a nightly study time."

If a child is doing well, conferences provide positive information that you can share with your child. If the student is not doing well, the conference provides the setting for discussing ways to solve the problem.

A few words of advice from teachers:

1. *Be prompt and stay within the time of your conference.* Schedule another time to meet or talk by phone if necessary to finish the conversation. Teachers, especially new teachers, may be reluctant to tell you your time is up.

2. *Write down ahead of time what you want to ask or to share with the teachers.* This will prevent the common post-conference reflection, "Oh, I should have asked about...."

3. *Talk about the important concerns you or the teachers have.* Save small talk for the end, if time permits.

4. *Show appreciation for the teacher.* Even if you have disagreements, remember that the teacher is working hard to provide an education for your child. A teacher will be more receptive to concerns if you are an ally rather than an enemy.

5. *Don't blame yourself for the child's problems.* While we all can learn much about helping our children and improving our parent-child interactions, problem-solving between parent and teacher should be the focus. Ask "What can we do to help Sarah?" instead of "Who's at fault?"

Parent Volunteer Opportunities

Parents are increasingly being encouraged to take part in their child's class or school. Some parents even say, "I'm afraid to attend the open house because they'll get me for something! I'm too busy already!" A corresponding comment is, "I feel bad when the teacher asks for drivers to field trips. Because I work, I can't be involved in class activities." Both comments have some validity, but they overlook two important points. First, involvement in our children's education should be on the top of our busy agendas. If we're too busy for this, then something else should go. Second, there are many ways to become involved today, even for working parents.

Parent volunteers accomplish more than just helping the teacher or school. On a personal level, they are showing interest in their child, and by giving of their time they are affirming the importance of the child's education. Furthermore, volunteering gives parents an opportunity to enjoy and share the school experience with their kids.

Parents of Southside Christian School, Holland, Mich., constructed this reading loft as a tree house in the school's media center. Children use it as a creature-friendly place to snuggle up and read.

Although teachers often ask for specific kinds of help, here are some possible ways you can offer assistance.

1. *Drive for a field trip or chaperone a class outing or party.* If you work during the daytime, ask what activities will occur in the evening. If you have young children, ask if they may come along.

2. *Be a classroom assistant,* offering to tutor, read with students, grade papers, prepare a bulletin board, or administer make-up tests.

3. *Provide food or supplies for a class*

party or trip even if you cannot attend the event yourself. Or, participate in school improvement projects.

4. *Help with the school play or musical event* by offering to sew costumes, apply makeup, set up chairs, sell or collect tickets, or assume clean-up duty. You will brighten a teacher's day by saying, "I see you have a Christmas or holiday program coming up. How may I help?"

5. *Join the Parent Athletic Group*, often called the Booster Club, and assist with athletic events. Parents can sell tickets, food, souvenirs—all to raise money for athletic events. They also often sponsor social events such as "meet-the-coach" times for parents.

6. *Ask the teacher how you may help*. Don't worry about being unable to do what is asked. Be honest about your availability as well as capabilities. Everyone can do something. You will receive far more than you give by sharing in your child's school world.

Attendance at School Events

"Did you see the long list of basketball games? How will I ever attend them all?"

"Wouldn't you know it! The Christmas play is on the same night as our office Christmas party! Of all the nights in December they could have chosen, they had to pick this one!"

"We received a letter from the teacher inviting parents to a reading party. What on earth is that? Of course it's during the day. Do I ask for time off from work and irritate my boss, or do I skip it and disappoint my child?"

Sound familiar? These are typical problems for most families. How do we attend so many events? Where do we draw the line and refuse? While each family will need to consider its own circumstances and make its own decisions, I believe that the more interest we can show in our child's school life, the better!

For single parents, those with young children or other care-giving responsibilities, and those whose schedules are already crowded, here are some suggestions.

1. *See if it would be possible to trade babysitting services so you and another parent each can attend some events.*

2. *Ask someone else—a grandparent, aunt or uncle, neighbor, friend—to attend in your place.* A side benefit is that more people will become involved in the school.

3. *Alternate who attends events*: mom or dad or even big brother or big sister. Sometimes you may even need to split the time between two events. I remember shuttling between two soccer fields to alternately watch my son and daughter play their games.

4. *Ask how other parents are dealing with this issue.* Perhaps this could be brought up at a class meeting.

PTA or PTO

Parent-teacher associations or parent-teacher organizations differ from school to school, and they certainly differ from the monthly meetings many older parents may remember from years ago. Schools have found it increasingly difficult to get parents to attend these functions, and many have reduced the number of meetings. Some schools have found alternatives: a family potluck followed by a meeting, a seminar day at which parents attend sessions on relevant topics, or a worship service for parents and teachers.

The value of a PTA is that it brings parents and teachers into social contact at a friendly, conversational level. It reinforces joint ownership of the school and educational process. It also creates an atmosphere that puts parents and teachers at ease in each other's presence, which can pave the way for more serious discussions about a child.

These opportunities for parental involvement—open house, parent teacher conferences, parent volunteer opportunities, attendance at school events, and PTA meetings—vary in their degree of focus on a specific child. Some foster parental involvement in the child's school while others focus on the education of the child. All are important and necessary. However, some additional parent-teacher contacts should also be considered.

Contacting the Teacher

Even if you participate in all available opportunities, you may still wonder about personally contacting your child's teacher. While teachers vary in their responsiveness to phone calls and contacts after school hours, it is entirely appropriate for you to call the school and ask the teacher to return the call. It is also appropriate to send a note and request a response. A teacher once said, "If you have a concern that you want to share with me, then I think it's important for you to call or send a note. I do want to hear from you!" It may be a good idea to ask the teacher at the beginning of the school year how and when he or she can be contacted. Some teachers establish dialog journals which children carry home and teacher and parent may write back and forth to each other.

Of course, some parents have taken the opposite approach—continual calls and contacts. While most teachers show concern for each child's needs, parents need to remember that there may be twenty-five other children with parents to whom the teacher must also respond. Ask yourself, "If I were the teacher, how would I feel about the number of calls and contacts regarding this child?"

Dropping In

Another source of concern is parental visits to classes. Carol, a beginning teacher, arrived at school one morning to find Mrs. V. waiting for her. Mrs. V. announced that she wanted to sit in on the class for the day. Carol was uneasy but did not dare to send the parent away. It was not a good day for visiting due to some schedule changes and anticipated interruptions. Carol made it through the day, but she regretted that Mrs. V. hadn't called to schedule her visit in advance for a mutually convenient time.

From this experience parents and teachers can learn a lesson. Teachers may want to set up visitation days and invite parents to sign up. While drop-in visits may be encouraged in some schools, they can make beginning teachers uneasy and disrupt classroom schedules.

While few parents may arrive unannounced for a whole day, many do drop in to have a word with the teacher before, after, or even during class. Drop-in chats should be kept to a minimum and should never interrupt a class during instruction. What may seem like a few spare moments to a parent may, in fact, mean the loss of preparation or instruction time for the teacher. Furthermore, if several parents drop in for chats, the lost time for the teacher adds up.

Therefore, it is best to leave a note, asking the teacher to call or to set up an appointment. Save drop-in chats only for urgent matters of immediate importance!

Parent-Teacher Communication

Finally, it is important for both parent and teacher to approach each other in the true spirit of communication. Parents and teachers talk and listen to each other; they write comments and read each other's concerns. This is what sharing is all about! There are three steps in communicating.

1. *Practice active listening.* Really listen to what the teacher is saying. Repeat or paraphrase what the teacher has said, so you can be sure you understand each other. For example, "So you feel that Johnny should be spending more time studying for tests? Are you suggesting that he doesn't appear to do homework carefully?" As parents we sometimes become defensive. It's better to first absorb what the teacher says.

2. *Use I-Messages.* Take ownership of concerns, and avoid attacking the teacher. For example, "I've noticed that Johnny has twenty-five math problems each night and it takes him an hour. I've wondered if this is a lot for his age. Perhaps you can help me here." Some parents react instead with a frontal assault, "Johnny spends an hour just on math each night. Why are you giving so much homework?" This puts the teacher on the defensive and prevents good communication.

3. *Engage in problem-solving.* Active listening and I-messages set the stage for parent and teacher to brainstorm ways to help the student. Each has something to contribute. For example, the teacher may respond to the homework statement by saying, "The twenty-five problems should not take more than 30 minutes. I, too, am concerned that he is taking so long. I'll watch him do some problems in school to see if he knows his math facts well enough to do the longer problems quickly. Could you observe him at home to see if he spends any of his math homework time daydreaming?"

Let's remember that the strength of our children's education comes first of all from God's blessing upon our efforts to raise our children in the way of the Lord. Let's also recognize that the strength of many schools is directly related to the extent of parental involvement in the school and collaboration with the teachers. God's will is done when we work together to further the training of his children.

Scenes from a Christian School Classroom

"How does a Christian school classroom differ from a public school classroom? Here are some scenes that capture the essence of Christian Education."

Parents face a daunting task in deciding whether to send their children to Christian schools. Many factors enter into their decision: proximity to the school, cost, quality of education, size, provisions for children with exceptionalities, and other practical matters. Some parents consider more philosophical issues: Shall I separate my child from the world? Should I support my community and its school?

Whatever parents decide is a family matter, entrusted to parents by God. The following scenes may help parents envision what a Christian school might be like. Let's visit some classrooms to discover some distinctive features of schools that claim the name of Christ.

What really is distinctive about a Christian school? That's a question often posed by parents who struggle with tuition payments, transportation arrangements, and other challenges when sending their children to a Christian school.

I recently visited five Christian schools and kept a journal of what I observed in kindergarten, first grade, and second grade classrooms. I saw many examples of Christian teaching and the pervasive influence of a Christian world-and-life view in those classes.

Prayer

In one school the teacher, Mark, began the school day with devotions. He shared a story about how God had helped him during a difficult time in his life, and he invited the class to join him in a prayer. "We can all say the name of a special person at the same time," he explained. "God will hear them all and know the needs of each person." When he said, "God, we ask you to be especially near to these people today," a chorus of names arose.

Sue wanted to help her kindergartners become comfortable with praying in front of class. When she invited anyone who wanted to say a sentence-prayer to come forward, eight students did. She encouraged the reluctant students to participate by standing next to the volunteers and giving them a few words to add to their prayers.

Songs of Praise and the Christian Life

After prayer many classes had a time of singing. Students in Karen's class were eager to meet their new letter person of the week, Mr. H., but Karen stressed the importance of starting each day with God. She lead the class in praise songs and then moved into the hippo song for Mr. H.

In Mary's classroom, the song "My Friend is Your Friend" related to the Bible verse that she read: "My command is this: Love each other as I have loved you" (John 15:12). Mary talked about Jesus' love, and then students walked around the classroom, nodding or smiling at class members as they sang.

Scripture and Bible Stories

In Christian schools Bible stories and devotional readings are found in abundance. Judy's class was learning verse 23 of Psalm 73: "I am always with you; you hold me by my right hand." She explained the verse and marveled at God's love for us.

Praising God is a hallmark of Christian education.

Heather wore a Noah's ark vest, which illustrated the Bible story of that week. She distributed booklets she had made for each child to illustrate. Their literacy activities centered on the Bible story.

Heidi was teaching her class to appreciate differences among people. She read a devotional from *Keys for Kids: Daily Devotionals Using Children's Bible Hour Stories* that stressed love, one of the fruits of the Spirit that her class was studying. Then she wrote four letters on the chalkboard, leaving space after each one: G___ L___ A___ P___. Students guessed at the missing letters in the words and eventually came up with God Loves All People. Heidi talked about how God made each of us different in order to create a beautiful human bouquet. From the Book of Revelations she read, "I looked and there before me was a great multitude that no one could count, from every nation, tribe, people and language, standing before the throne and in front of the Lamb." She read this passage (7:9) to show the students that all types of people belong to God's kingdom.

Sherry's class completed the statement, "Love is. . . " by drawing pictures. One student drew four children sharing play equipment and waiting to take turns. Below the drawing was the verse, "By this all men will know that you are my disciples, if you love one another" (John 13:35).

Discipleship

A hallmark of the Christian faith is responsible discipleship: believers are

Students in Zeeland Christian School, Zeeland, Michigan, demonstrate Christian friendship.

to follow Christ by helping others. The verse, "Be kind and compassionate to one another, forgiving each other, just as in Christ God forgave you" (Ephesians 4:32) had an impact in the schools I visited.

In Nellie's classroom a small group read aloud together at a comfortable pace so that the slower readers were helped by stronger readers. Meanwhile, the rest of the class paired off for activities on the computer, in the art center, or in the poetry corner.

Students demonstrated kindness even to a stranger. While I was observing a group taking turns reading in Sheri's class, one boy offered to share his book with me. He pointed to the line of text so I could follow along—evidently thinking that I couldn't read.

Stewardship of Creation

Another mark of Christian faith is taking care of God's creation. Ruth's students adopted a dove as a class pet, which in the Bible symbolizes God's presence. Students took turns taking care of the bird and talking to it to make it "feel at home."

Using a sunflower theme, one class planted a garden so that students could learn first-hand about their responsibilities to God's creation. The teacher emphasized the theme by creating a bulletin board that proclaimed "Planted in God's World."

Students at Southside Christian School, Holland, Michigan, created paper sunflowers to resemble the sunflowers growing in the school garden.

Supportive Christian Communities

Parents are interested in and involved in the activities at Christian schools. For example, in the South Side Christian School library in Holland, Michigan, parents built a magnificent reading loft in the shape of a tree house complete with a tree trunk in the middle (See figure in previous article, "Parents and Schools"). Students could climb a few steps and sit to read books in the company of stuffed animals. At Hudsonville (Michigan) Christian School parents monitor lunchtime and recess once a week so that teachers can meet in grade-level groups to have devotions and share teaching ideas.

Christian Conduct

Many classrooms displayed posters with rules for conduct such as Mary's Club Rules: Attentive Listening, Mutual Respect, Soft Voices. However, teachers also realized that students don't always show regard for others, especially on the playground. Tricia handled conflicts by having a message box in which students could place notes expressing their concerns.

In one class the teacher used instances of misbehavior to talk about the influence of sin. She explained that when sin entered the world through Adam and Eve's disobedience, it hurt all of God's creation, and we deal with the results everyday. "Now for the good news!" she announced. "Jesus' death on the cross has conquered sin! That means that we can ask for forgiveness for our sins. We can ask for help with our problems, and we can do our best to live like Jesus every day."

Recognition of Differing Needs

The teachers cited in this article loved each student as God's child, created in his image with talents that can be used to serve him and others. The challenge for them was to find ways to meet students' individual needs, recognizing that children differ in ability, achievement, and developmental levels.

These teachers had several ways of meeting the varying needs of their students. They often set up groups so that students of different abilities could work at their own pace. They were careful to keep the groups flexible and to organize topic and interest groups as well as ability groups. Teacher aides, volunteers, parents, and grandparents provided valuable help to these groups.

Sheri and Renee acknowledged the different developmental levels of their kindergartners by showing them the various ways that children their age write: with pictures, with single letters, and also with words. Several teachers encouraged the students to write in their journals and assured them that they would all be able to do grownup writing someday.

Could some of these examples of caring and consideration be found in public schools? Certainly. But taken together, the scenes presented here provide a window into Christian school classrooms. In the Christian schools I visited, a Biblical perspective comes across in so many ways.

We need to pray for our teachers in both Christian and public schools, in the schools our children attend and in the other schools in our communities. Perhaps the best support that we can give a teacher is to say, "Here are the skills I have and the times I have available. How can I use them to assist you as you teach my child?"

Developing
Responsibility
for Life
and Learning

Allowances:
To Give or Not to Give –
That is the Question!

"Is there one right answer to the question of an allowance? It is one of the many issues on which parents must reach a decision, determining what is best for their family."

"We decided to give Jane a weekly allowance," said Mr. O'Conner. "That way she can learn just how far money goes (or doesn't go!) today. It teaches her to budget her funds, and it allows her to make decisions about the things she wants to buy. Before Jane got an allowance, she was always asking us for money for this or that. I was always put in the position of deciding what I thought was worth financing. Now she has to decide. Starting an allowance is one of the best things a parent can do!"

Mrs. Harrison sat listening patiently to Doug O'Conner's enthusiastic speech. When he finished, she asked for a chance to present her view.

"Let's hear it," responded Doug, as the rest of the parent group listened attentively.

"None of my children receive an allowance," Liz Harrison began. "My husband and I discussed the issue several years ago when our son claimed that everyone he knew got an allowance except him. Of course, we discovered that he wasn't the *only* one in his class who didn't receive an allowance, but he was one of the few."

She continued, "We decided that, rather than hand over a certain amount of money weekly, we would rather have our children ask us when they need money. Then we can decide if it is a worthwhile expenditure. I think it gives children too much freedom to provide money for them to use as they please."

"How do you feel about letting children earn money for doing chores around the house?" asked Mrs. Hatcher, another parent in the group. "Let me give you an example. My husband and I both work, and we were discussing hiring a cleaning person for our house. Our teenage son asked us to hire him and we did. It's worked out beautifully. He knows that if the cleaning isn't finished, he doesn't get paid. I think this helps introduce him to the world of work."

Is there one right answer to the question of an allowance? Probably not. It is one of many issues on which parents must reach a decision, determining what is best for their family. What about Christian families who have the covenantal responsibility to bring their children up in the fear of the Lord? Again, there doesn't appear to be one right answer. Obviously, the subject of allowance is not directly discussed in the Bible, but there are three scriptural principles which set a general tone for the Christian's attitude toward money. First, the Bible clearly cautions against dishonest monetary acquisition (Proverbs 13:11, Matthew 27:5, Luke 3:14). Second, the Bible explicitly states that "the love of money [not money itself!] is a root of all kinds of evil" (1 Timothy 6:10, see also 2 Timothy 3:2, and Hebrews 13:5) and can interfere with serving God (Matthew 6:24, Luke 16:13). Third, the Bible reminds us of the source of our material wealth by requiring that a portion of our earnings should be returned to God (1 Corinthians 16:2). Any money which we or our children acquire is subject to these considerations. And we must teach these principles as part of our covenantal responsibility.

How are Christian parents dealing with the issue of children's spending money, specifically allowances? In an attempt to find out, I conducted a small, informal survey in a Christian school in the Grand Rapids area. I spoke with 190 students in grades 3, 6, and 9, asking about sources of spending money, work requirements, and parental guidelines for the use of their money.

What Families Do

When asked if they receive a weekly allowance, 83% of third graders, 67% of sixth graders, and 53% of ninth graders said they do. More than 80% of those receiving an allowance indicated that payment of the allowance depends upon completion of household chores or family responsibilities.

What are the chores or responsibilities these students are expected to complete? Third graders reported such obligations as care of family pets, table setting and clearing, taking out trash, cleaning their rooms, making their beds, and assisting parents with laundry, cleaning, yard work, and child care. Many indicated other sources of income such as help to grandparents in their gardens, taking neighborhood children for walks, or helping siblings with paper routes. Several students who do not receive an allowance earn money within their families by completing specific jobs such as dusting, picking up around the house, or cleaning the basement. One student indicated that coins were hidden around the house which could be found and kept while he did the dusting.

Sixth graders reported many of the same chores in order to earn their allowances. In addition, they have a higher level of responsibility, such as care for a younger sibling, mowing the lawn, cleaning the car, washing dishes, or emptying the dishwasher. Again, many students who do not receive an allowance are paid for jobs around the house. In addition, there are several other sources of income: paper routes, lemonade stands, and chores for neighbors or grandparents.

Ninth graders still are responsible for many of the same kinds of chores as their younger schoolmates. However, a few trends can be noted at this age. Ninth graders often have a cluster of family responsibilities like taking out the trash, mowing the lawn, and cleaning their bedrooms or setting and clearing the table, doing the dishes, and dusting. It's

Courtney Cone sweeps the floor, showing us that even young children can do chores.

also interesting to note that only about half of the ninth graders surveyed received an allowance, in contrast with approximately 2/3 of sixth graders and more than 3/4 of third graders. This is probably related to a third trend: 87% of ninth graders reported outside sources of employment. The three most frequently reported "jobs" are babysitting, mowing lawns, and delivering newspapers. Thus, a decrease in allowance may result from new sources of income.

Several students in each grade reported that they do not receive an allowance but are permitted to ask parents for money when they need it. It is more common for younger students to be given money upon request, while older students are usually expected to "earn" funds.

As might be expected, there is a diminishing amount of parental guidance as students get older. Nearly all third graders, the majority of sixth graders, but only a few ninth graders reported some type of parental control over spending money. Most of the students in all three age groups reported that parents expect them to return a portion of their money to the

Lord through church, Sunday school, or other Christian causes.

Although this survey was limited to one school system, it's safe to predict that many of the patterns would hold true in other schools as well. In many Christian homes, allowances are being given; most children are working for them; and allowances diminish as outside sources of income increase. Parental guidance for spending money is strong at young ages but weaker as children get older, and expectations exist for returning a portion to the Lord.

Advice from Parents

What suggestions would parents give to those considering the question of allowances? Here is a sampling of parents' opinions:

"An allowance gives a child a specified and limited amount of money for which to be responsible."

"An allowance permits a child to decide among many uses for the money and teaches the lesson that we can't buy or do everything we want."

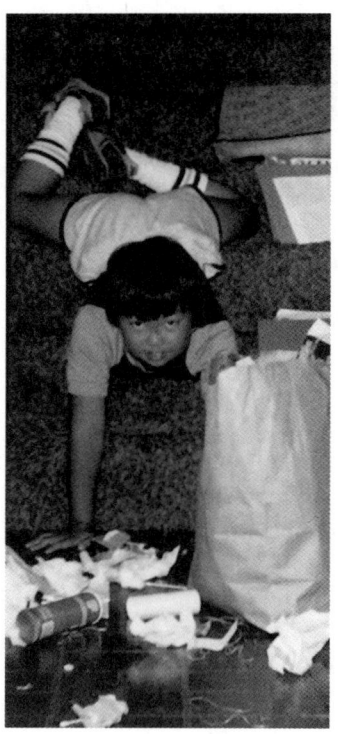

John earns an allowance for emptying the wastebaskets. This time, however, the trash tumbles down the stairs ahead of him!

"An allowance which depends upon performance of chores teaches a child that one must work for money. Remember the old saying, 'Money doesn't grow on trees.'"

"Payment for services around the house is an early introduction to the world of work. It should be phased out as the child is able to obtain outside sources of employment."

"An allowance with parental guidance at a young age enables parents to teach children some principles for money management."

"The principle of tithing or returning a portion of money to the Lord is made very concrete for children when they have their own money to give."

"Paying children for jobs around the house gives them an honest means of earning spending money."

However parents decide to answer the allowance question, they should keep in mind the biblical principles regarding wealth. All that we have comes from God, and we must use it wisely and well to his glory and for the benefit of our neighbor, whether we are 8, 10, 14, or 40.

Raising
Responsible
Kids

*"Developing a sense of responsibility in kids
is a primary goal of all parents, but it sometimes
seems like an impossible dream."*

"How can I get Jeff to make it home on time for supper?" asks MaryBeth.
"We bought him a watch for his birthday, but he still doesn't get home at 6
o'clock. He learned to tell time in second grade, but now it seems as if he's
forgotten!"

"Aisha never picks up her clothes. She leaves them where they drop after
she takes them off. I can't stand to go into her bedroom. I've done everything I can to make her be responsible," complains Joyce.

"I ask Justine to watch her sister for one hour while I give piano lessons," says her mother. "But when I return, Ariel's often gotten into something, and Justine is mesmerized by the TV. Last week Ariel got into the
laundry detergent—what a mess!"

Developing a sense of responsibility in kids is a primary goal of all parents, but it sometimes seems like an impossible dream. Nevertheless, parents are to train their children to love God and their "neighbors." As children mature, they must develop a sense of responsibility to themselves, to
others, and to God.

Responsibility to Self

Young children are egocentric. The world revolves around them, and they
see the world from their perspective. They think everyone else sees the
world the way they do. Wise parents tie in the development of responsibility to their child's level of maturity.

The young child's accountability can begin with picking up toys, often
with help from parents. The main idea to stress is that these are the child's

toys, so he or she must keep them safe. Young children can also pick up their clothes, brush their teeth, and wash their hands.

Toddlers often want to help with household chores. Two-year-old Micah has seen his mom and dad put away the groceries. When he helps with this task, he puts boxes and cans in various cabinets, but not the right ones. Tamika wants to help with the wash. She sees a tub of water and decides to wash her doll. After she immerses the doll, she pulls it out and lets water drip all over the floor. Although this kind of "help" can be exasperating for parents, kids will develop a sense of responsibility as they participate in household chores. The time that parents spend with Micah and Tamika will be well worth it.

When I had two toddlers at home, they typically spread their toys all over their bedroom and the hall. We didn't bother to pick them up at night, because the next day the kids would haul them all out again. We just learned to step around them.

One night my husband explained to the girls that somebody could accidentally step on a toy and break it. Were there any toys they didn't care about? "No!" they answered emphatically. Once they understood the possible consequences of leaving their toys out, they decided that putting them away would be worthwhile. My husband also explained that one of us could get hurt stepping on a toy. While this was true, the possibility of losing a treasured plaything seemed to have more impact. Young children react to what most directly affects them here and now.

Children seem to learn best when responsibility is a joint venture. Telling a toddler to pick up his or her toys or to get ready for a bath may not produce instant obedience. But helping the child and gradually reducing the amount of assistance you provide will help the child become independent. As kids become more competent, you can gradually assign them more complex and challenging tasks. For example, your son might begin by placing the napkins around the table, but as he gets older, you can ask him to set out plates and silverware.

Responsibility to Others

As children grow, they can differentiate themselves from others and from the rest of the world. While we may train a young child to be kind to others and to respect the person and property of others, a slightly older child can begin to appreciate how others feel, to empathize and sympathize as well as to envy and resent. When kids are in the elementary grades, help them develop a sense of responsibility to and for others. Caring for younger siblings, participating in household chores, handling other people's possessions carefully, and treating other people with respect are appropriate and realistic goals.

Ironically, even though kids are increasingly able to help with chores, they also seem increasingly reluctant to do so. The young child who wanted to set the table becomes the fifth grader who exclaims, "Do I have to?" You might answer that barring a sudden illness or emergency, the table must be set. If the child shirks responsibilities, she will have to face the consequences.

School also gives children an opportunity to develop responsibility to others by collecting milk money, feeding the pets, watering the plants, or serving as the teacher's helper. Parents should commend teachers who structure classrooms in a way that complements what you are trying to do at home.

When children approach adolescence, some parents mourn the passing of the cooperative, or at least partially cooperative, helper who accepted and carried out responsibilities around the house. The preadolescent or adolescent may master the art of dodging responsibilities, to the despair of parents who thought they had made great progress in the first 10 to 12 years.

"Kim was the most reliable nine-year-old you could ever imagine," claims her father. "She begged to take her brother for a walk, to feed him, and to bathe him. We had to limit her because we didn't want her to burn out. She also loved to set the table for supper and to help make salads. Now that she's 13, she can hardly say a civil word to her brother, she complains whenever she's asked to do something, and her room—well, that's something else."

The adolescent is moving from parental reminders to independence in doing assignments, studying for tests, planning for extracurricular events, and scheduling time for social activities. Teenagers often sandwich family responsibilities in between what they see as the really important events in their lives. We may remind teens who act as if family obligations are beneath their dignity that responsibility to family doesn't end in high school.

Courtney Cone learns about her responsibility to her own body by learning to brush her teeth.

Parents sometimes tie the privileges that teens request to their assigned responsibilities in the family. Unfortunately, some teens accomplish tasks only at the threat of losing the car for the weekend or being grounded.

An important part of the adolescent's responsibility involves avoiding premarital sex and substance abuse. Home and school work together to help teenagers develop respect for their bodies as temples of God, to be kept holy and pure. A variety of parental support groups have sprung up to offer help and encouragement for parents of teens. Peer counseling, Young Life, and Students Against Driving Drunk are a few of the programs that help students develop discernment to avoid irresponsible and often disastrous choices.

An area of increasing concern among parents and educators is the subject of work. For teenagers a part-time job can promote a sense of responsibility and emphasize the qualities that will be required of an adult in society: punctuality, using time well, learning new skills, communicating, and getting along with others. But a common danger today is that many teens are working so many hours that their schoolwork suffers. Although teen jobs may be commendable, they should not interfere with school.

Responsibility to God

The most important responsibility for all of us to develop is to our Creator. As parents, we promise God to train our children to know God and to serve him in the world today. The world begins at home. It spreads to church, community, and school, and eventually it leads beyond. We explain to our children where we intend our training to lead them. We enjoy acting responsibly before God, and we want them to also.

During family devotions we can read Bible passages that explain how people served God in their various tasks. We pray together as a family that we will honor God in our daily activities. When we make choices between courses of action, we explain to our children what we believe will please God.

In the family we move from taking responsibility for ourselves to taking responsibility for others, nurturing, helping, and supporting each other. Above all, we must foster a sense of responsibility to God, under which all other service can be subsumed.

Responsibility Begins at Home

1. *Start young.* Often we think that a child must grow up before participating in family obligations. But if you have patience with young kids when they want to help, you will nurture their growing sense of responsibility.

2. *Build upon beginnings.* As the child grows older, responsibilities increase. Emptying wastebaskets is followed by taking out the trash.

Courtney learns about her responsibility to others by helping her mom, Caroline.

3. *Reap the consequences.* In order to keep kids motivated to do their chores, you may have to establish rewards and consequences. Some parents give allowances based upon completion of family obligations. Kids also learn from negative consequences. For example, if they don't put clothes in the hamper, they won't have clean clothes to wear next week. If the bedroom isn't cleaned up, they may not have friends over.

4. *Fair isn't necessarily equal.* When ten-year-old Maria is assigned to vacuum the upstairs of the house and six-year-old John is assigned to take the newspapers out to the garage, the jobs are not equal in difficulty or time. However, what is fair is that both children are learning responsibility.

5. *Develop the "other" perspective.* Families face both a challenge and an opportunity to develop a sense of service to others, thereby also serving our Creator. An excellent idea is to take on a service project as a family.

6. *Develop a commitment to serve God.* A real commitment to God is something we should discuss in the family and ask God to help us develop. When talking about the day's events, suggest ways that a Christian can serve God in the midst of them.

The Study Battle:
A Necessary
Tug-of-War?

"'You said you didn't have much to do
and you insisted on playing and watching TV.
Now it's bedtime.'"

For children, the beginning of a new school year brings with it the anxiety and anticipation of new classes, new teachers, new friends, and maybe even a new school. For parents, it can mean a welcome return to a fairly predictable routine with children's daytime hours scheduled by someone other than Mom, Dad, or the neighborhood kids. However, in many homes a new school year means redrawing the battle lines in the combat over homework.

One mother describes it as a tug-of-war. She is on one end of the rope, pulling Johnny toward his homework. Johnny is on the other end, pulling toward his friends who are waiting at the door after school. Johnny promises to do his homework later and races out the door, leaving Mom holding the rope.

After supper, the tug-of-war resumes. Mom is still pulling toward homework, but Johnny is now pulling toward the TV. "I don't have much homework, Mom. Just one program first, please?" he begs. "Then I promise to get started!"

"O.K., just one program," agrees Mom. Soon, however, one program has turned into two or three. Mom returns, having reached the end of her rope. "Johnny!" she demands, "What about that homework?"

"Sorry, Mom. I'll do it right now."

The opening skirmishes have concluded, but the battle isn't over yet. Johnny begins his homework, but his pencil breaks and he leaves to sharpen it. Then he runs out of paper and goes in search of more. He notices the dog by the door and helpfully takes it outside. An hour passes, and five math problems are finished.

Parent Larry Louters assists his daughter, Julienne, with homework.

"How are you doing?" asks Mom encouragingly.

"Fine," is the standard reply.

"Are you just about finished? It's almost bedtime."

"Uh, I've still got about twenty math problems and a few history questions," Johnny barely whispers.

"How many is 'a few'?" Mom asks, trying to remain calm.

"Only about fifteen," answers Johnny, even more softly.

"What? All that work at this time of night? You said you didn't have much to do and you insisted on playing and watching TV. Now it's bedtime. You'll have to get up an hour and a half early tomorrow. Be sure to set your alarm!"

The tug-of-war has ended, but a winner cannot be declared, even though the rope seems to have broken.

A purely fictitious scene? Not at all. Similar battles are being fought—and lost—every night in North American homes.

Is the study battle necessary? Yes and no. "Studying is definitely not one of those things that come naturally to young people," says Ann Erickson of the International Reading Association's committee on parents and reading. While there are many students who are motivated self-starters, there are many more like Johnny who need some parental nudging. Ideally, a child should do homework independently, but the fact is that many children simply need help getting into the study habit.

Suggestions for Parents

To help your child acquire that habit, here are 17 STUDY STOMPERS to help you stomp out the study battle. These suggestions are aimed at elementary children, but most can be adapted to older students with some modifications.

1. *Guide the child in understanding that school work is a God-given responsibility.* Just as adults have responsibilities, so do young people.

2. *Plan for a study time every weekday afternoon or evening.* Schedules may call for varying the time, depending on music lessons or after school activities, but when possible keep the same time every day.

3. *Arrange for a place where the child can work undisturbed.* Some children insist that they work better with the radio on, and you can check their output to see if this is true.

4. *Ask your child what homework has been assigned and ask to see the assignment sheet.* Make it clear that you expect the homework to get done!

5. *Help the child make a plan for getting it done.* For example, your youngster may prefer tackling math first and saving English for later. Help your

Daniel Alderink gets a little help with his homework from his mom, Ellen.

child estimate the amount of time necessary for each subject.

6. *Assist the child in making long-range plans for major assignments.* A monthly calendar will help keep the long-term assignments from being forgotten.

7. *Check finished assignments and reward with praise, affection, or a treat.* Offer to help by reviewing the material for a test or quiz.

8. *For children with shorter attention spans, provide recognition or reward upon completion of part of the homework.* For example, you might say, "When your math is finished, show me the paper and we'll fix the snack you asked for." Or, "When you finish your history questions, you may take the dog for a walk."

9. *Praise any efforts that result in success, whether that success means a good grade or improvement over past work.*

10. *Encourage children who need to make better use of time to stick to a schedule by using a kitchen timer.*

11. *Empathize with the student when there is a large amount of work, but let the child know that life contains that sort of pressure for all of us at times.*

12. *Help a reluctant student with positive encouragement.* For example, you might say, "Let me help you get set up for reading this chapter. I can guess what you'll be reading about from this picture (or title)." You might want to check if the youngster understands the assignment. For instance, "Show me how you do this first math problem."

13. *Save a favorite TV program or activity until after all work has been done.* This gives the student incentive to finish the work on time and gives him or her something more appealing than just bed or a bath to look forward to.

14. *When time is at a premium, have another family member call out spelling words or questions in the car.*

15. *Allow time on weekends for catch-up work, when necessary.*

16. *Save some desk work of your own to do—letter writing, bill paying, school work— when the child studies.* Sit across from the youngster so that you work together.

17. *Keep in touch with the teacher about your child's work so that you can take corrective action before the report card comes home.* Also, speak to the teacher if the child seems to have an inordinate amount of homework, or too little.

School is a student's top priority and other activities must fit around a school work schedule. Sometimes teachers hear this lament, "But I don't have time for homework! Three nights a week I have swimming practice; Wednesday is family night at church; Tuesday is gymnastics." Students need to approach activities by asking the following question: "With the amount of time needed for school work, how much time do I have to participate in extra activities and which activities have top priority?"

One final word: students quickly discover their parents' ideas about school and homework. Showing the child that you take homework seriously and letting him or her know what you plan to do to help will go a long way toward establishing good study habits. As Christian parents, we are charged with encouraging our children to develop whatever talents they have and assisting them in carrying out their God-given responsibility. A little help can go a long way.

January Blahs
and Homework Blues:
Keeping the Momentum

"Bad homework habits may present an imposing challenge. . . Consider three types of students: the super achiever, the kid who needs some encouragement, and the procrastinator."

"Wake up and do your homework!" Dad exclaimed as Ned slouched over his textbooks one January evening after supper.

"But it's so hard to concentrate. I just can't get motivated!" Ned replied.

"That may be, but unless you get motivated, you won't be going to the pizza parlor this weekend with your friends! Work before play, you know." To Ned, a middle-schooler, his father's words of wisdom seemed to come from a distant time and place.

"I'm trying to help you get ready for high school and college. You can't save everything until the last minute and still get it done!" Dad was always practical and looking to the future.

A few blocks away, Jennifer, a high school student, was talking on the phone to her friend Michelle about tomorrow's history test. "I haven't studied at all yet. In fact, I haven't even finished the assignments. I've been babysitting so much that I just can't find the time to get everything done! And I need to babysit to pay off my Christmas debts. What a mess!"

"You could've done some of the assignments over the Christmas break," Michelle said. "Ms. Arnelle gave us all of the assignments early so we could be well-prepared."

"Oh sure, like I'm going to do homework over vacation. Get real!" Jennifer exclaimed.

"What are you going to do now?" Michelle asked.

"Who knows? Maybe I'll take a nap and hope that I wake up more interested in World War II than I am now! I always seem to squeak by. Just being in class is enough to do fairly well on the test," Jennifer answered.

It's January, and the blahs have arrived. January begins the longest stretch of the school year uninterrupted by holidays. Bad homework habits may present an imposing challenge for your kids in January and beyond.

But you can help your kids develop homework habits that will assist them in the future.

Three Different Students

Consider three types of students: the superachiever, the kid who needs some encouragement, and the procrastinator.

Michelle is a superachiever; she is actively involved in sports teams, music lessons, and church activities, and she seems to manage her busy schedule quite well. She gets her homework done on time, and she sometimes stays up late or gets up early to complete assignments to her satisfaction. She spends time reflecting on and perfecting her work. She is a self-starter. Even in January she can jump back in, eager and ready to work.

Next, there is the student who needs some guidance. Remember Ned? He

Homework Helps for Younger Kids

For families of young children who are just beginning to deal with homework issues and haven't yet identified a Michelle, a Ned, or a Jennifer, a general set of guidelines may be helpful. Here are some suggestions to consider.

1. Have kids complete all homework and household responsibilities by bedtime.

2. If kids consistently have trouble getting their tasks accomplished, work out a plan that they can follow.

3. Map out the week, and leave time in the schedule for homework and chores each day.

needs frequent reminders to do his homework. At the end of the school day he's ready for a change of pace, and he looks forward to hanging out with his friends. After supper he may postpone homework until he's seen a favorite TV program or two. He may need help turning off the TV and turning on to schoolwork, but eventually he settles down and finishes most, if not all, of it by bedtime. Before the holidays he was getting into a routine, becoming a bit more of a self-starter. But vacation left him in a relaxed mood. When school started up again, it seemed that he almost needed to start over.

Finally, there is the procrastinator. Jennifer listens to CDs or watches TV at a friend's house after school. She comes home for supper but often leaves to "do homework" at a friend's house. She also babysits two afternoons during the week and has practice for basketball three afternoons.

At bedtime, Jennifer usually discovers that much of her homework remains to be done. When her mom asks why she didn't start earlier, Jennifer claims that she had no time earlier.

Michelle, Ned, and Jennifer represent common approaches to homework. Most families have more than one type of student and have learned that

4. Since unexpected events may occur, allow for occasional deviations, possibly one per week. (Of course emergencies may change this, but the kids should realize that the plan is serious business.)

5. On a no-homework night, schedule free reading time. Setting aside a regular time allows kids to discover "forgotten" homework and promotes reading development.

6. As much as possible, plan for the whole family to share homework times: parents can pay bills or read the newspaper while children do their schoolwork. Parents also can quiz kids on spelling words, look over math problems, or ask about the books kids are reading.

7. January is a good time to review your family's involvement in activities. Is your family overly busy? What are your priorities as a family, and what do you need to set aside until another time?

8. January is also a good time to think about some fun family activities to beat the blahs. Maybe this would be a good time to start planning your summer vacation.

9. Finally, January is a good time for your family to review your commitment to God, making sure there are regular times of devotions and recognizing that God gives us the ability to accept responsibilities and to meet commitments.

treating kids exactly alike produces unsatisfactory results. But parents also know that being fair doesn't necessarily mean treating children equally. Indeed, some kids need more help than others when it comes to assuming responsibilities and accomplishing them on time.

Advice for Michelle

I have met many Michelles in college. Frequently they are the first-born child in their family. They want to do everything and be the best at everything. They may manage a hectic pace in high school and try the same in college. But in college there is more of everything—more studying, more social interaction, more distractions, and perhaps more hours at a job to help pay tuition.

Michelles easily become stressed out and frustrated. You can encourage them to establish a pattern of schoolwork, employment, and other activities that will help them in subsequent years. Here's what to tell Michelle:

1. *Choose from among the many activities you want to be involved in* rather than trying to do too much. Develop a schedule.

2. *Be satisfied when you've completed a paper or assignment well* rather than continuing to revise and perfect it.

3. *Give yourself some personal time to relax and to avoid that frazzled feeling*; you'll enjoy everything more.

4. *Figure out what things need to be done first*, and don't try to do everything at once.

5. *Work to achieve balance in your life* so you can be involved in some of the things you like, but not to the extent that you feel stressed with all the demands on your time.

Advice for Ned

We have many Neds in college, both male and female. Typically they enjoy college very much, seeming to major in activities and minor in studies. They spend their freshman year pulling all-nighters to do the studying that didn't get done during the day because of sports practice, participation in a club, or too much socializing. Neds also later regret the effect that this approach to homework has on their grade point averages.

You can help Ned deal with time management problems in middle school that could become major problems later on. This is what to tell him:

1. *Follow "Grandma's rule: no dessert until you finish your mashed potatoes."* Save a preferred activity until you complete some homework or a chore.

2. *Use a schedule sheet or calendar to plan each day's time*, and stick to it quite closely.

3. *Realize that there will always be distractions that seem interesting or fun.* You need to make choices.

4. *Reward yourself for a week of getting your homework done on time* by doing a favorite activity on the weekend.

Advice for Jennifer

Jennifer is another type of student we often see in college. She sees college as a yearlong youth convention: lots of fun, little sleep, many activities, much social interaction, and, of course, some class attendance and occasional studying. Jennifer is finally away from parental reminders and can do her own thing. She'll work late at night, all night if necessary. In the morning, she may skip classes, but she tells herself that at least she gets some assignments done. She sees the time between classes as free time to eat and visit with friends. She finds the dorm distracting, so she goes to the library where she manages to get just as distracted by like-minded students. Jennifer can be helped during her pre-college days to establish better habits. Here's what Jennifer needs to hear:

1. *"Grandma's rule" applies*—school-work and responsibilities before activities!

2. *You may lose privileges if you don't get your work done*, earn poor grades, or cause problems in class.

3. *Avoid excuses for failing to get work done*. We can all find a reason for everything, but it's better to face the problem head-on.

4. *Realize that you're setting a pattern for life* that will affect your future school and work habits.

5. *Keep working at it!* We can't correct bad habits overnight, but persistence pays off. Many students have turned their study habits around and are successful and proud of the results.

The next few weeks of school can be significant ones for your children. You can help them by recognizing the January blahs and by setting guidelines for getting homework done and enjoying school.

Facing
Special Needs
in Educating
Children

Is My Child Gifted?
Don't Be Afraid To Ask

"I'm sure a lot of parents think their children are gifted;
if Donny is gifted, his teacher would say something.
I don't know whom to ask."

Donny is a six-year-old first grader who reads at the fifth-grade level. He loves science, and his concerned teacher, together with the librarian, has developed a package of books for him. He loves to read the Hardy Boys mystery books and often reads one from cover to cover in a couple of hours. He is very curious, asking numerous questions at home and at school, and he loves to do experiments and discuss them.

But Donny does poorly on his school assignments. He has two approaches: hurry, get it done, hand it in, and get it wrong; or ignore it, look around, fiddle with a paper clip, or sneak out a book to read. Whichever choice he makes, the paper goes home to be finished or gets done during recess. Donny rarely writes neatly; his letters are crooked and poorly spaced.

Donny doesn't mind working on a paper during recess because he doesn't enjoy playing with other children, nor they with him. To his classmates, Donny seems to be in another world, always looking for insects and leaves or making something from twigs or rocks. To Donny, the other children don't seem to want him. "Why don't they like to do the things I like to do? Why don't they ask me to join their games?" he wonders, but he is generally content in his own little world.

Donny's mother, Mrs. Moore, an articulate and well-educated woman, hears him tell me a story for some reading research I am conducting. Donny recounts a lengthy, complex episode about a rabbit with no friends. The rabbit travels far and wide, asking an assortment of animals to be his friend. Donny includes all the elements that are associated with a fable or folktale: setting, initiating event, internal response of the main character, attempts of the character to reach a goal, consequences of the character's attempts, and resolution of the conflict. When he finishes and returns to reading,

Micah and his kindergarten friends explore a science program on the computer. Wisely chosen computer programs can assist parents in providing for the gifted.

Mrs. Moore asks to speak with me. She is almost in tears.

"I know Donny was telling that story about himself," she says. "You see, he doesn't seem to relate to other children his age, and they don't ask him to play. Even on the corner, while waiting for the school bus, he is ignored, sometimes even teased."

"I've another concern," she adds and then tells me about his reading, his work habits, and his interests. "I think he may be gifted. He seems very intellectually advanced for his age. His teacher is willing to work with his high reading level, but I still think there's more that he needs in a school program. His poor performance on worksheets—is it because his fine motor skills aren't developed, or is he just bored?"

She continues, "I'm sure a lot of parents think their children are gifted; if Donny is gifted, wouldn't his teacher say something? I don't know who to ask. All the children in our neighborhood are bright, and if I speak to a neighbor, she'll think, 'Who does she think she is, suggesting her son is gifted? My Sarah is every bit as smart as Donny. She's reading on an advanced level, too.' So you see the predicament I'm in."

Mrs. Moore is not alone in her dilemma or her perception of the way others might react. It seems that parents can safely mention all types of exceptional needs—learning disabilities; mental or physical impairments; hearing, speech, or visual limitations—and receive a response of interest and understanding. But let parents suggest their child is gifted, and other parents regard them as snobbish. Teachers also may react the same way, seeing parents as ambitious, idealistic, or opportunistic. It should not be so, especially among people of faith in both Christian and public schools, who acknowledge that each child is a child of God, created in his image to fulfill his purpose.

What should Mrs. Moore do? She should ask Donny's teacher about the referral process for having him tested. If the teacher is reluctant, Mrs. Moore should discuss with her the reasons why and perhaps speak with the principal. Many schools do their own testing, and Christian school parents often have such services available through their local public schools. Private testing is another alternative, provided that such testing includes an evaluation of a child's educational needs. In any event, this family has a right to know their child's abilities, his strengths as well as his weaknesses, so that an appropriate educational program or additional opportunities outside of school can be arranged, if warranted.

Defining the Gifted

What is a gifted or talented child? In a report to Congress, former U.S. Commission of Education, Sidney P. Marland, representing the United States Office of Education, offered the following definition: "Gifted and talented children are those identified by professionally qualified persons who by virtue of outstanding abilities are capable of high performance. These are children who require differentiated educational programs and services beyond those normally provided by the regular school program in order to realize their contributions to self and society" (Marland, 1972). This definition became the benchmark for organizing programs.

The same report by Commissioner Marland goes on to identify the areas of giftedness proposed by the Office of the Gifted and Talented. Six broad areas of giftedness include: general intellectual ability, specific academic aptitude, creative thinking, leadership ability, and visual and performing arts ability, and psychomotor ability. In each case, the child's abilities are consistently superior to those of his or her classmates, and in each case, the student would benefit from specially planned educational services beyond those normally provided by the standard school program.

Let's return to Donny for a moment. We might suspect that he will show general intellectual ability, specific academic ability in reading and possibly other areas such as science, and creative thinking. We do not know about visual/performing arts, and we might guess that he does not show unusual ability in psychomotor areas or leadership. In fact, we might suspect areas that are not well developed here. Gifted children can be gifted in some areas and not in others.

Nevertheless, Donny does show characteristics which warrant further investigation. He may need more intellectual stimulation, assistance in social interaction, help with psychomotor tasks (such as the fine motor requirements of doing a worksheet), and/or alternatives to worksheets. His mother's concern is real and well-founded.

What should she do? First, she should speak up and find out. Then she should investigate what special programming is available in school, what adjustments can be made in the regular classroom, and/or what opportunities outside of school may be appropriate. Parents and schools need to work together to meet the needs of each child, to consider what can realistically be done, and to seek outside help as needed.

Multiple Intelligences—a new dimension

Recently much attention has been paid to the theory of multiple intelligence suggested by Howard Gardner (1983). Gardner proposed at least seven intelligences: linguistic (verbal), musical, spatial, logical-mathematical, bodily-kinesthetic, interpersonal (understanding of others), and intrapersonal (understanding of self) (Gardner, 1989, 1993). To these he has now added naturalist and a ninth is proposed— spiritualist (Farris, 2000). Implications of Gardner's theory for schooling suggest that teachers teach in a way that enables students to learn according to their strengths. The goal is that learning can occur in a number of ways, commensurate with the various intelligences. Teachers should also allow multiple and diverse expressions of learning that enable students to use their intelligences in demonstrating their learning.

Developing Abilities

Parents have the right to ask that their children be evaluated for giftedness, as they do for disabilities. They may ask how the school is helping children develop in the area of the multiple intelligences, too. But they should also be realistic in recognizing the limits of what a school can provide. Frequently, parents need to provide some of the stimulation or enrichment for their children outside of the school environment in their children's areas of giftedness or intelligence, through either private or public opportunities. Here are some examples:

Music lessons, church and community choirs, junior symphonies, and music-in-community programs.

Ballet, dance lessons, sacred dance, and local performing arts programs for children.

Nature center and zoo programs, museum activities, as well as nature exploratories with parents using guidebooks to supplement their own knowledge.

Mentor programs with experts in various fields through schools, colleges, and businesses.

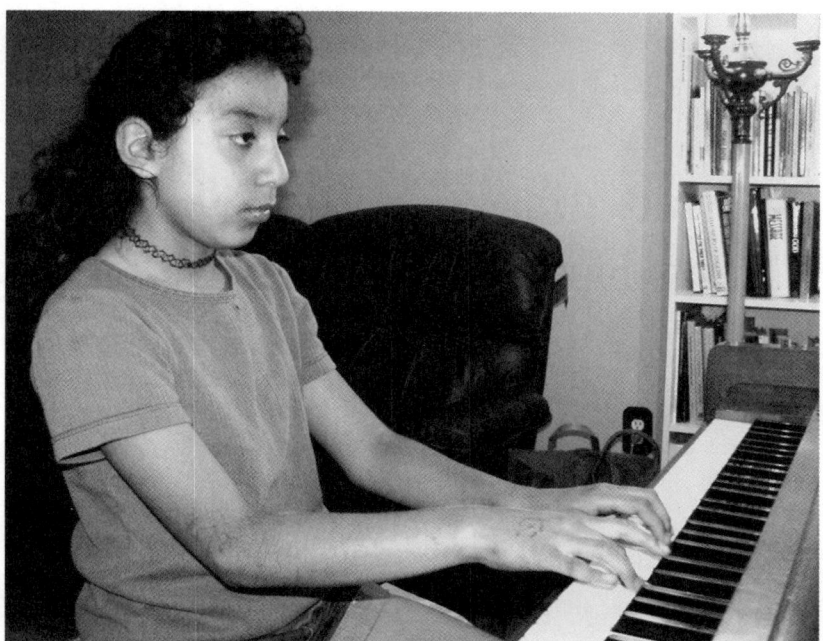

Emily Alderink concentrates on her piano lesson. Piano and music lessons provide children with enrichment outside of the classroom.

Club involvement in church-affiliated groups like Gems and Cadets, Girl Scouts and Boy Scouts, local Girls and Boys Clubs, and Bible clubs.

Summer "camps," sponsored by colleges, schools, or city recreation departments, such as chemistry camp, foreign language camp, sports camps, computer camp, etc.

Community and church sports teams: soccer, football, basketball, and baseball.

Debate teams, spelling bees, poetry groups, young authors' festivals, and local or state writing contests.

Computer programs and CD-ROMs in children's literature, reading and math skills, science and history adventures.

The above examples are just some of the many opportunities that may exist for parents to help their children develop in areas of giftedness or multiple intelligences. One word of caution is advised by teachers: Take care not to overcommit your child. We see too many "hurried" children and frazzled parents today. Choose what works best for everyone in the family!

No Matter How Worthy: Do Parents Have Unconditional Love?

"Loving our kids and helping them learn to see themselves as God's children means that we should never ask 'Do they deserve our love?'"

"Jesus loves me, this I know..."

"Jesus loves the little children, All the children of the world..."

These children's songs are sung often in vacation Bible schools, Sunday school classes, Christian school classrooms, and around the house. Who are these children we sing about, how do they view themselves, what are their goals, and how will we help them attain these goals? What sort of influence can parents have on their children's goals, their view of themselves, their approach to the circumstances in which they find themselves, and their striving to succeed or their giving in to failure?

Parents often see intelligence as the ticket to a child's success in life. The first thing parents look for in a child—after determining whether she has all ten toes and fingers and whether her complexion is rosy—is how intelligent she is and will become. Parents are keenly aware of the ages at which a child should acquire language and motor abilities. They are delighted if their son or daughter reaches a milestone early, but they are fearful and disappointed if a child is a little behind, taking a few extra weeks to say "Mama."

Mom and Dad can do much to influence a child's likelihood of success or failure, but the stage can also be set for unrealistic pressure on the child. A youngster has to live up not only to his own expectations, but also to the expectations of his parents, no matter how high they may be. Not all children are Mozarts, able to compose symphonies at a very young age, or Edisons, who invent many new things and strive for excellence. The vast majority are, as Christian psychologist James Dobson suggested (1979, 1999), just plain kids who need to be loved and accepted as they are.

---

*This article is co-authored by Arden Ruth Post and Karen Rigotti

God created children in his image. As parents we show God's love for us in the love we have for all of our children.

Every parent hopes for children with exceptional talent. But that's just not going to happen, and most of us come to terms with our children's abilities and disabilities, strengths and weaknesses, just as we have had to accept our own. We learn to love our kids as they are and teach them to love themselves, just as we've learned to accept ourselves as we are.

But some kids present a special challenge in loving and accepting them as they are. These kids also need extra help in accepting and loving themselves. In a society that places a high value on intellectual ability and academic success, many students fall far short of even attaining average grades. Yet Jesus loves them, and he would have us love them too.

All children need to develop positive feelings about themselves because God created them in his image and for his purpose. Let's examine four types of children who may pose a special challenge to parents to accept them and to foster positive self-acceptance—the mentally impaired, the learning disabled, the physically handicapped, and the gifted underachievers.

Rory

Rory began school when he was five. After a year of kindergarten, the school recommended that he repeat kindergarten because of immaturity and lack of readiness for first grade. His parents agreed. After entering first grade a year later, he was unable to acquire the beginning reading and math skills and was finally referred for testing. The diagnosis came back that he was mentally impaired. Although the teacher presented the information in a considerate, understanding, and helpful manner, there was no escaping the verdict. Rory was impaired, and his parents were crushed.

How could this happen? Father and Mother were college graduates. Two older siblings were already in college. While Rory's parents had noticed some slowness about him, both intellectually and physically, they expected him to outgrow it. He was always a challenging kid, and they couldn't wait for this tag-along to grow up. Now they feared that he never would.

Meanwhile, Rory was beginning to notice that he was different from other children. Everyone was reading books while he was still learning letters. Kids were playing games at recess which he couldn't follow. He began to hang around his teacher for comfort. She was nice to him. She even said some nice things about him which surprised him. With his classmates and at home, Rory felt rejected.

At home Mother and Father had trouble accepting Rory. They feared that soon everyone would know they had a impaired child. They became harsh with Rory: forcing him to try to read, making him stay outside to play with neighborhood children who didn't want him, berating him when he couldn't catch a ball, and insisting to the school that he stay in the regular classroom.

Rory's already low self-esteem plummeted. He cried, wet the bed, got sick, and made his parents angrier. And the worse Rory felt about himself, the worse he did in school. He didn't feel like a child created in God's image; instead, he felt rejected, lonely, and stupid.

Susan

Susan was in the fourth grade. She was called a miracle child by her parents and teachers because she was born prematurely with a weight of only three pounds. When Susan progressed to the point that her life was no longer threatened, her parents began to watch carefully for signs of impaired development. But testing seemed to indicate above average intelligence, and her parents breathed a sigh of relief.

However, Susan's progress in school lagged considerably behind that of her classmates in several areas. While the other fourth graders were perfecting cursive writing, Susan continued to have trouble with manuscript printing. Her letters slanted in all directions, rarely touching the line. She reversed b's and d's, p's and q's. Spelling was purely phonetic: *they* was *tha*, *river* was *rivr*, *rice* was *ris*. She seemed unable to remember sight words for either spelling or reading. When reading aloud, she sounded out each word laboriously. She also reversed several words, so that *saw* became *was* and *on* became *no*.

In math Susan was a whiz at computation. She passed her timed tests in multiplication and division and was working on some advanced problems. But her math skills didn't keep Susan from feeling dumb. She was painfully conscious of her limitations in reading and writing.

Susan's parents—a lawyer and a former teacher—were clearly disappointed. Exasperated, they had Susan tested again and, although her intelligence was still above average, she showed signs of a learning disability. Fortunately, Susan had a concerned teacher who worked with a learning disabilities specialist to create opportunities for Susan to succeed and to build up her self-concept. But a fragile ego was being destroyed at home, and no amount of school intervention could compensate.

Barbara

Barbara was a little girl with cerebral palsy who walked with canes or crutches. She was always pleasant, and her classmates liked her. Barbara had average intelligence, but she was behind her classmates in achievement due to absences for several surgeries on her legs. Also, Barbara changed schools several times as her parents sought the best educational setting for her.

Barbara's parents struggled to provide as normal a life as possible for her. In fact, Barbara seemed to get along so well at school that her parents viewed her as just one of the kids in the class. They encouraged her in physical activities, sometimes beyond her endurance. When her dad played ball with Barbara's brothers and sisters, she was expected to play too. Her parents expected her to do just a little more homework than her classmates so she could catch up. They asked the teacher not to accept sloppy work even though the teacher believed Barbara's best effort would not reach her parents' standards.

In school, Barbara began to cry a lot, refusing to do some work. On the playground she became bossy, and classmates began to shy away from her. The teacher believed Barbara felt insecure, possibly from too much pressure to be normal physically and to achieve academically. In a conference with Barbara's parents, the teacher suggested that Barbara should be given more time to catch up in school work and be allowed to hand in less-than- perfect papers. She also expressed concern that Barbara's self concept, which seemed to be very positive in spite of her handicap, was beginning to suffer and that Barbara was beginning to dislike herself.

Mark

Mark was an extremely bright boy. He had a fantastic memory, was very articulate, showed amazing creativity, and had a keen sense of humor. He was also bored with school, put forth the least amount of effort possible, earned C's and D's, and couldn't care less, or so it seemed. At home he was happy-go-lucky, but totally irresponsible and undependable. His parents were utterly frustrated. Mark's dad worked in a local factory and was saving to send Mark to college. Mark's mother was puzzled. Why would a boy with so much ability not want to use it to get somewhere in life?

Mark's carefree attitude often got him into trouble at home. His parents believed he should spend more time studying, and they often reminded him.

Deep down, Mark knew he could do better in school. His grades did make him feel bad, and he began to dislike himself, becoming more resentful, not only of his parents but also of himself. His happy-go-lucky nature was becoming a facade for a worsening self-concept.

Rory, Susan, Barbara, and Mark represent four types of children frequently found in our families and our classrooms. While each has a different set of problems threatening both self-concept and academic achievement, each needs to feel acceptance, love, and support at home and school to stand a chance of success.

Children Share Common Needs

Rory, Susan, and Barbara share common needs. First, they need to be accepted as they are. Regardless of what we do to help them, if we don't feel good about our children, they won't feel good about themselves.

We also need to make certain that they are in an appropriate educational setting, with a combination of the regular classroom combined with special education assistance. The setting should challenge them to use their abilities and also set realistic expectations for achievement.

The teacher and school atmosphere are as important as the setting itself. A caring teacher can pave the way for the child with special needs to be accepted by other children, creating opportunities for both academic success and a positive self-concept.

Every child has some areas of talent. The special-needs child particularly needs to be helped to develop the areas in which he or she can shine. But areas of weakness or limitation cannot be ignored. Perhaps a tutor or therapist can be engaged to help with educational, emotional, or physical problems. Parents should also seek advice from professionals or counselors in the appropriate field to find out specific information about the child's disability, what to expect in terms of achievement, how far to "push," what strengths to build up, and how to effectively help, not hinder, the child.

Mark, a high schooler, presents a very different set of parenting challenges, yet he needs as much love and support as Rory, Susan, and Barbara. Mark's parents need to confer with his teacher about realistic expectations for his performance and the kind of structure they can set up to foster positive work habits. Mark also needs a set of short-term goals along with rewards for reaching them. For example, if he completes his homework all week, he may go out Friday night. If not, he stays in until it's finished.

Mark's teacher should be enlisted to help find challenging and motivating work for Mark. In addition, both Mark and his parents may benefit from counseling. His parents want to know how to handle him, and Mark needs help in developing the motivation he wishes he had.

Can we as parents and members of the Christian community truly say that we love our children, all of them? Do we accept what we can't change about them? Are we willing to provide support to help them change what can or should be changed? Are we helping them develop good feelings about themselves? And finally, by our words and deeds, our acceptance and support, are we cherishing them as children made in God's image to fulfill his purpose for them on his earth?

Love One Another

"Even at a time when accommodations are made and services provided for those with disabilities, we want to be 'normal' and to associate with those who are 'normal.' Exceptions and exceptional people can make us uncomfortable."

She was an attractive, little girl with her long hair pulled neatly back in a ribbon. She entered the doctor's waiting room, calling out to the receptionist. "I'm Jenny White and I'm 10 now!" she said, smiling.

"Hi, Jenny," said the receptionist, "the doctor will be ready to see you soon. Meanwhile, you might like to play with our new toys."

It was then that I could see the difference as Jenny faced me and walked toward the toys. Jenny's face gave the first clue. Jenny's choice of toys and the way she played with them seemed to confirm my thoughts. She appeared to be a child with Down syndrome.

Jenny began to put together the brightly colored plastic animals. Soon she had one of the animals chewing on a nearby plant. "Keep the animals on the table, dear," said her mother, and Jenny obeyed.

At this time two children entered the waiting room with their mother. "We have some new toys," said the receptionist, and the children went over to the play area. They looked at Jenny, playing contentedly. "Want one?" she asked, holding out an animal to the children. They stepped back. "Wanna play?" asked Jenny. The children moved toward their mother, who was also looking at Jenny and frowning.

"Get another toy and play over here," was their mother's whispered advice. Jenny looked puzzled for a moment; then she went on playing alone. Jenny's mother sat with her hands folded, looking down at her lap. Such an occurrence may not be common in an era of greater acceptance, but it still occurs for the exceptional child or adult. Those of us who have exceptional persons in our families or who work with them can probably relate many incidents similar to Jenny's experience.

Even at a time when accommodations are made and services provided for those with disabilities, we want to be "normal" and to associate with those who are "normal." Exceptions and exceptional people can make us uncomfortable. But aren't there some exceptions that we admire? Of course. For example, a teenager might say, "Bill is such a great athlete. If only I had his talent, I could be captain of the basketball team too. Think of how popular I'd be!" Or a father might say, "If I had my boss's brains, I could be president of the company too!" Or a mother might think wistfully, "I don't know how Susan Smith does it! She keeps a beautiful home, is a gourmet cook, has well-mannered children, *and* she has a terrific job. I guess some people just have what it takes!" Most of us admire exceptional characteristics such as athletic prowess, intellectual ability, and efficiency, among many others.

But let's consider the larger realm of exceptions. Just who is the exceptional child or adult?

- the young man living down the block who walks with an uneven gait due to cerebral palsy?
- the boy next door who is an inclusive education student, whose schooling consists of a mixture of a regular classroom and special education?
- Jenny, the girl in the doctor's office, who functions on a younger developmental level than her age would suggest?
- the emotionally disturbed teenager who is withdrawn or given to outbursts of rage?
- the girl in fifth grade who receives special help in reading and math because of a learning disability?
- the electronics whiz who's always coming up with a new gadget?
- or how about the brightest kid in school, who gets all A's year after year with little effort?

All of these people may be considered exceptional. Their unique needs may require the following adaptations in education programs to provide optimal learning conditions: classroom modifications for the physically disabled, a slower-paced, concrete learning experience, training in occupational skills, counseling and a therapeutic educational environment to work through problems, remedial instruction capitalizing on strengths and addressing areas of concern, an enrichment program in areas of exceptional ability, or accelerated subject area classes.

But what does this mean for the rest of us? We probably support special education programs and community, state, and agency assistance for the physically and/or mentally impaired. We may also support Christian educational facilities like Elim Christian School in Illinois, Pine Rest in Michigan, or Salem Christian School in California. What more can we do?

Perhaps the simplest, yet most important thing we can give is our love. It requires no money, yet it is something we all have. With love we can take a step further and promote positive, caring relationships with exceptional persons.

A bulletin board at a Christian school declares, "All God's children are special!"

Acceptance and Appreciation

Love begins with an attitude of acceptance. The exceptional individual is a person first, and exceptional second. As Christians we have often heard Jesus' words, "My command is this: Love each other as I have loved you" (John 15:12). This verse is easier to apply to those who are like us or who have characteristics that we admire. The more a person differs from us, the more difficult it can be to love and appreciate that other person. Appreciation suggests that we go beyond mere acceptance and admire truly unique and special qualities with which God has endowed each of His children.

It's valuable to remember that all of us have some degree of exceptionality or disability. We may wear glasses; we may struggle over math or science or spelling; we may sprain muscles and break bones. Our disabilities may be permanent or temporary. The point is that we can think of a continuum of abilities and disabilities within which each of us falls. Consider that persons with mental impairments differ from others in the degree to which their learning capabilities enable them to pursue school work. Their disabilities may also limit their choice of vocations, but certainly not exclude them from the world of work today. God has given all of us a certain type and range of abilities within which to work in his world.

Is the socially or emotionally disturbed person also similar to us? Yes, because most of us can identify times in our lives when circumstances seemed to conspire against us or when life seemed to bring us more than we were able to cope with, leaving us depressed or upset. We may have sought help from a pastor or a professional counselor to cope with problems. It's only the duration or the degree of disturbance that differentiates us from a person considered socially or emotionally disturbed.

At this point you may agree but still believe, "I am surely different from a brilliant person." Not necessarily. Many gifted and talented people excel in a single area: academic work, visual or performing arts, a technical field, athletic ability, or an area of creativity. Every school, church, community organization, or social group contains ample evidence of the diversity of God's gifts. Psychologist Howard Gardner's (1983, 1989, 1993) emphasis on multiple intelligences suggests that there are many areas of giftedness. We all possess the possibility of further developing many areas in ourselves and others.

Now let's consider people with physical impairments. Yes, some children and adults live with impairments so severe that we marvel at their ability to cope. We can be thankful for well-functioning bodies. If a broken limb has slowed us down for a time, if arthritis kicks up now and then, or if we live with a chronic illness, we may have some notion of what it's like to live with a physical impairment. Again, it is only the degree or duration of disability that makes us different from the person who is physically impaired.

Relating to Persons with Exceptionalities

Exceptional individuals are more like us than different from us. They have the same needs that we have: to feel loved, to be safe and secure, to have family and friends, to achieve as much as he or she is able, and to be

Kim Woudenberg, a member of Shawnee Park Christian Reformed Church, Grand Rapids, Michigan, and a participant in the Friendship Series, celebrates her 30th birthday with her family and church friends.

accepted. It is these needs that we can help to meet. How?

- by showing the same love and concern for an exceptional person that we show to each other.
- by greeting the child with Down syndrome as we would greet another child.
- by asking the adolescent with mental impairment how school or work is going just as we would ask any other teenager.
- by rejoicing with the child with a learning disability, who has learned some math facts just as we would rejoice with the senior who received a college scholarship.
- by showing a special interest in and concern for the child or adult with social or emotional problems.
- by including young adults with disabilities in the life of the church and the community.
- by making special provision for people with physical impairments to attend church, school, and social functions.
- by visiting a family where a particular impairment prevents an individual from going out; or, better yet, by offering to spend a morning or evening with the individual so that his or her family can pursue an activity.

In short, we need to include the exceptional person in our world of friends and in our love for one another.

Perhaps a starting point is to ask, "How would I react to a Jenny White in the doctor's office? How would I encourage my children to react?" This may be a good topic for family discussion at the evening meal.

When God created us, he made us in his image. He made us unique, with diverse talents and abilities. He has a purpose for each of us, even if we are disabled. We have seen that exceptional individuals have much in common with us. We also remember God's command to love one another. Then let us regard each brother and sister as our equal in Christ, love each one with the love God has shown us, and impart this attitude to our children.

A Case History:
Meet David,
A Disabled Reader

*"Reading disability is complex, offering various combina-
tions of symptoms and requiring unique combinations of
approaches."*

Meet David, a handsome child with chestnut brown hair and dark brown
eyes. He speaks clearly, using sentence structure and vocabulary beyond
what might be expected for his eight years of age. He is excited today and
eagerly asks questions about the reading clinic where his parents have
brought him to be evaluated.

David has just completed second grade at a Christian school. He has had
a traditional reading curriculum: learning letter names and the sounds of
consonants in kindergarten, and beginning a basal reading program in grade
one. The basal reading program included children's readers at various levels, workbooks, and activity sheets. Basals provide a comprehensive approach to learning to read: word attack skills including phonics, sight words
to be recognized immediately, vocabulary words to reinforce word meanings and comprehension questions. David's school added its own phonics
program to give students an extra dose of the sound-symbol connection.
The teachers also use much children's literature.

Most of David's classmates are experiencing success in reading, many of
them reading material that is several grade levels above second grade. In
addition to learning to read in school, these successful readers read all the
time. Some of them seem to read everywhere—in the car, in the yard, in
every room of the house, even while eating in a restaurant.

David prefers other activities. He rarely reads books because they are
hard and there are too many words he doesn't know. He especially dreads
being called on to read in class or for devotions at home. He makes errors,
someone laughs, then he makes more errors, and on it goes. "If only schools

© David Buffington, PhotoDisc

didn't have reading," David thinks, "and spelling and writing, too." The rest of school is all right and, of course, recess is the best part of the school day.

Before considering David's specific problems, a word needs to be said about diagnosis. There ought to be a sign in every diagnostic reading setting stating, "Diagnosing reading disability can be hazardous to your health." There are several reasons for this. First, any kind of labeling can make a child wonder, "What's wrong with me?" It can sound like an illness. A label can lead to the feeling that one is a lesser individual. Often, the label, while describing a condition, may also ensure that the condition perpetuates itself, a self-fulfilling prophecy.

Second, diagnosis is worthless unless a remedial program is planned based on the results of that diagnosis. Examples can be cited where a battery of diagnostic tests were performed, sent to a school, only to take up permanent residence in the child's file after the principal and teacher have given them a cursory glance.

Third, parents often plead, "If only we knew what's wrong with him, we could fix it. If we know what he has, there must be a specific cure." Unfortunately, reading disability isn't like appendicitis where the source of the problem is easily removed and recovery is almost guaranteed. Reading disability is complex, offering various combinations of symptoms and requiring unique combinations of approaches.

Analyzing Reading Behavior

Reading teachers and specialists use the term "reading behavior" to analyze and describe how a child handles the reading process. Rather than focusing on what's wrong, we look at how a child reads orally and silently on lists of words and in reading passages. We check comprehension of facts, word meanings, and inferences derived from a story. We check oral reading rate and types of oral errors, evaluating whether or not they deter comprehension. We investigate the child's performance in the broader area of language arts—spelling, writing of sentences and paragraphs, English grammar and usage, handwriting, and oral language. We use some formal, but mostly informal tests, because they tell us what we need to know. What is the essence of what we are looking for? The child's strengths and areas of concern in reading and related language arts areas. We expect to find both strengths and areas of concern, and we always do! David's diagnosis was not confined to the information obtained during his visit to the clinic. It included information obtained from parent and teacher questionnaires, past school records and previous testing, as well as observations, testing, and trial teaching, done at the reading clinic. The following were determined to be strengths which David brought to the reading task:

- a happy disposition, likes working with people, relates well to adults and children
- motivated to read better, willing to work
- excellent oral language including a large vocabulary, fluent speech, and good sentence structure
- strong comprehension in all areas evaluated: facts, word meanings, and inferences
- likes to read when books aren't too hard

The following areas of concern were also uncovered:

- laborious word-by-word oral reading
- uses only one strategy to figure out an unknown word: sounding it out
- takes a long time to sound out words, repeating sounds many times
- needs to figure out too many words, which is why reading is so slow and laborious
- slow reading rate, orally and silently
- confuses similar words, such as *want* and *went*, *where* and *were*

Is David a disabled reader? Probably, if we use the term to describe someone whose reading behavior indicates certain areas of concern that inhibit his ability to make appropriate grade-level progress in reading instruction. But to give David such a label is valuable only if it is necessary for him to obtain specialized instruction from a reading specialist or resource teacher.

We will use the term with utmost care! Criteria differ among schools for providing remedial assistance. Public schools often have more programs available than private schools, but they may also have more stringent criteria for qualifying. It is entirely possible that David would not fit the criteria for remedial help in some public schools.

Christian schools are increasingly adding reading or resource teachers to provide for students such as David. They frequently have more flexible entry requirements into remedial programs. Whether David can get help will depend on how many others also need help and the severity of their problems.

There are a wide variety of approaches to take for remediation for a student like David. The important consideration is to choose a combination of strategies that will address his particular strengths and areas of concern. A word of caution to parents is to be wary of any remedial setting that applies the same strategy to all disabled readers. Just as ill people don't all need the same medication, so disabled readers don't all need the same prescription.

Planning a Program

In planning a program for disabled readers, teachers and specialists aim at the areas of greatest need. Here are some suggestions for a reader like David.

1. Connect reading, writing, listening, and speaking as much as possible. David will see reading as part of communication, not just trying to pronounce words correctly.

Specific technique: The Language Experience Approach (LEA) (Stauffer, 1970; Allen, 1976; Vacca, Vacca, and Gove, 2000) to teaching reading can be used by the classroom or remedial teacher. Parents can use a modified form at home. One of David's strengths—speaking—can be used to do the following:

a. Have him dictate a story.

b. Print it as he says it.

c. Read it back to him.

d. Ask him to read it silently.

e. Ask him to read it orally.

f. Use the story for learning words, comprehension, drawing illustrations, etc.

This technique has proven to be very effective. It is based on the following theory: What I think, I can say. What I say can be written. And my words that are written, I can read.

2. Teach David more words as whole units. He needs to recognize more words immediately upon seeing them. This will help him gain fluency in reading. Sounding out too many words takes too long and becomes frustrating. Furthermore, many words can't be sounded out and need to be memorized visually.

Specific technique: The Visual-Auditory-Kinesthetic-Tactile Approach (VAKT) can be used by the remedial teacher, the classroom teacher, or an aide. It is helpful for children who are weak in auditory and/or visual learning because it adds additional senses: movement (kinesthetic) and touch (tactile). Parents can use a modified form at home by following these steps for teaching sight words in reading or spelling words:

a. Write the word in large letters with black crayon, preferably on newsprint paper. The LEA story mentioned above is a good source of words to pick out for learning.

b. Say the word.

c. Trace the word with your index finger over which you have placed your middle finger. Say it again while tracing it.

d. Do this a few times.

e. Invite the child to trace and say.

f. Tell the child that when he thinks he knows the word, he should turn the paper over and write the word.

g. After he writes it correctly three times, he writes it on an index card to be saved for review.

3. Give David carefully chosen practice in oral reading. Often disabled readers are made to sit with parents to practice reading. This can be frustrating for parents who wonder, "Why does he sound so bad?" and for children who wonder, "Why can't I read like my friend Sean?" More harm than good can be done by these nightly recitations.

Specific techniques:

a. *Silent reading should come before oral reading.* Always allow David to read material silently before reading orally. Encourage him to ask you to pronounce any unknown words, or simply point to a few that seem hard and pronounce them for him. Read silently as he does and when you're both finished, ask him, "Read aloud the sentence that tells. . . ." This technique requires him to read for a purpose, to search through a passage, and then to read aloud a small amount. Encourage him to ask you a question that requires you to read aloud to him, too.

b. *Use the tape recorder.* Obtain some Bill Martin Predictable Readers, like *Brown Bear, Brown Bear, What do You See?*, which contain appealing, easy books and a tape. A child can read along with the voice on tape and then read on his or her own. As an alternative, assist David in taping himself as he reads. Then ask him to listen and talk about what he'd like to improve. Then let him read it again, once or twice. Children are often excited to hear themselves improve.

c. Make oral reading fun at home!

• Read to him, letting him supply certain words, like character names, as you point to the lines. For example, in Goldilocks and the Three Bears, he can be asked to say the names: Baby Bear, Mother Bear, Father Bear, and Goldilocks as they appear in the text, or read their dialog.

• Take turns reading sentences. Frequently, parents have a child read a whole page, and then the parent reads a whole page. This can be too long. Read together in unison. Reading aloud together allows you to model reading and gives him immediate support. It is always more comforting to do something together than to do it alone.

These are only a few of the suggestions for a reader like David, intended to suggest the type of remedial program that could be developed. It should be stressed, however, that each program is different, and early diagnosis is crucial to the development of an effective program.

Note: *The Read-Aloud Handbook* (1979, 1995-3rd revised edition) by Jim Trelease gives delightful suggestions of books and techniques. Trelease also published *Hey! Listen to This: Stories to Read Aloud* (1992) and *Read All About It!: Great Read-Aloud Stories, Poems, and Newspaper Pieces for Teens and Preteens* (1993), focusing on grades four through eight.

Signs of a Possible Reading Disability

Disabled readers differ in the kind and severity of symptoms they exhibit. Frequently, a young child will exhibit a few of the following characteristics but not have a reading disability. For example, reversing letters such as *b* and *d* is common in young children and should not, in and of itself, send parents to a reading clinician.

The list is given as a guideline for parents who may want to contact the teacher or principal if they see a number of these characteristics in their child.

1. *Short or erratic memory for words.* Words that others seem to learn easily are difficult for the child to remember even after they have been seen many times. The child may know the word one day but not the next day.

2. *Hesitant, word-by-word oral reading.* The child may read so haltingly that an adult observer feels like saying, "Just spit it out!" Naturally, beginning readers may read this way at first. Therefore, a child's teacher can best judge whether the child is experiencing an unusual amount of difficulty in this area for his or her grade level.

3. *Difficulty learning phonics.* Phonics refers to the sound-symbol correspondence between the written and spoken word. It is the strategy we mean when we say, "Sound it out." There are some children who have great difficulty learning phonics and continue to labor over sounding words out, for example, *t-ree, c-a-t,* long after their classmates have put these words into their sight word knowledge which they recognize immediately.

4. Confusion of similar words in reading and spelling. When parents call me to talk about this problem, I know exactly which words they will say: *want/went/what, there/where/were, this/that, on/in, an/and, tree/three,* etc. It appears that some children (and adults) have difficulty concentrating on the differences among similar words and remembering the differences over time.

5. Reversals of letters or words. Often this characteristic is overrated. However, in combination with other characteristics, it may be important. Reversals may take several forms: letter reversals: b/d, p/q; word reversals: *saw/ was, bad/dab, on/no,* or partial word reversals: *ant/nat.*

6. Overuse of phonics. Some children use only one strategy to figure out unknown words: sounding it out. While this is a valuable strategy, it is by no means the only way to figure out an unknown word. Schools are often partially to blame for this problem for two reasons: (1) phonics can be given so much time and attention that it almost appears that phonics = reading; (2) other strategies are not taught. A very useful set of strategies is found in context clues: surrounding words, sentences, or pictures that suggest what an unknown word is. The child is encouraged to finish a sentence and return to the word to check on the guess.

7. Concern about oral reading performance. The disabled reader tries hard to sound good and equates a good reader with one who reads fast and fluently. While few teachers or parents think they are having students perform when they call on them to read aloud, this is exactly what is happening. Any error is quickly corrected by teacher or parent or the child is told to sound it out. Reading groups, in which round robin oral reading occurs with children being called upon, can be a nightmare! Oral reading needs to occur *after* children have had a chance to read silently.

Oral reading should be done for a purpose such as, "Look back to find the name of the dog. Put your finger on the sentence that answers this question. Now read that sentence." This is good reading practice for all children, and the disabled reader needs to learn that there is more to reading than sounding good.

8. Attention and concentration deficits. Frequently, disabled readers do not pay as much attention during classroom instruction as their classmates do. Their ability to concentrate, to stay with a task, is often lacking, too. Reading specialists often wonder how many of a child's reading needs are due to the fact that the child wasn't paying attention during instruction or persevering during practice.

9. Difficulties in other areas of language arts: spelling and writing. Rarely is reading a child's only problem. Usually, the language arts area is affected more broadly so that we see the following:

a. Spelling is very phonetic. Words to be learned by visual memory are often sounded out and thus spelled incorrectly.

b. Sentence structure shows incomplete or run-on sentences.

c. Handwriting is immature for grade level.

d. Organization of written work on a page is difficult. Frequently the child has difficulty placing the name, date, listing of numbers, or paragraph indentations, in the correct place

e. English grammar/usage shows omissions and incorrect usage. The child may place capital letters here and there but not consistently where they should be. Punctuation is also sporadic. It seems as if the child knows he must use periods and commas but places them anywhere.

10. Achievement in other academic areas and non-academic areas is higher than in reading/language arts. Disabled readers frequently do well in math and non-reading areas. They may be very adept at manual skills, building things, taking things apart, and reassembling them.

If you have been concerned about your child's reading and have seen some of the above symptoms, contact your child's teachers first, to ask their opinions. Then go to the principal if you remain concerned. You may wish to request an evaluation by your school or your public school district. Be sure to ask for a complete reading evaluation, if possible. Fortunately, there are ways to help all disabled readers. David is eager and ready to have someone unlock the keys to reading for him. How many other Davids are out there waiting?

Lance—LD, RD, or Just a Kid with Learning Problems?

"Mrs. Taylor had learned through her years of experience and her training that students who produced papers like Lance's were not just lazy or in a hurry. A paper like Lance's indicated real learning problems."

"Look at that paper! What a mess! Can't you do any better than that? We've got a tutor for reading; it looks like we need one for writing, too!"

Lance's mother was beside herself. She couldn't believe the problems her son was having with schoolwork. First, he had problems with reading, and the school got him help from a special reading teacher. His parents hired a reading tutor also. The next year the school advised moving him into a special class because he needed help with several subject areas. She knew she shouldn't yell at him, but she was exasperated. Where would it end?

Frequently, a disabled reader has problems in areas other than reading. This is frustrating for parents, students, and teachers. Often the related areas of language arts—spelling, handwriting, grammar and usage, speaking, and listening—show evidence of difficulty too. In fact, parents and teachers sometimes wonder whether the child is learning disabled.

Reading Disability or Learning Disability?

There are probably as many different explanations of the distinctions between these terms as there are specialists in these fields. One explanation is that a reading disabled child has difficulties only in reading. Disabled readers are defined as having a discrepancy between their potential ability in reading and their actual reading achievement. Disabled readers frequently have broader problems in other language arts or content areas also.

A learning disabled child is usually considered to have a broader range of problems. The learning disabled student is often described as having normal to superior intelligence while exhibiting a discrepancy between ability and achievement in one or more of the following areas: oral expression, listening comprehension, written expression, basic reading skills, reading comprehension, math calculation, or math reasoning. While both definitions use a discrepancy to define the disability, the definition of learning disability typically allows for more subject areas.

A constellation of characteristics may accompany a reading or learning disability. One or more of the following may be evident:

1. *Short or erratic memory for words.* Recognizes few words by sight. Needs many exposures to a word in order to remember it.

2. *Hesitant, word-by-word oral reading.* Laboriously plods through a story.

3. *Difficulty learning phonics.* Can't seem to connect sound and symbol or has trouble blending sounds into a word, *c-a-t.*

4. *Confuses similar words in reading and spelling:* what/want, then/when, etc.

5. *Reverses letters or words in reading and writing:* b/d, saw/was, and/nad.

6. *Overuses phonics in figuring out unknown words.* Tries to sound out almost every word.

7. *Attention and concentration deficits.* Seems inattentive in class during teaching. Doesn't stick with a task during independent work.

8. *Difficulties in other areas of language arts:* spelling, writing, English grammar and usage.

9. *Achievement in other academic areas and non-academic areas is higher* than in reading/language arts.

Unfortunately, the debate will probably continue over the difference between reading and learning disabilities, and the particular students who fall in each category. In reality, a student's classification is frequently determined by two pragmatic considerations: what specialists a school has available, and for which services a student will qualify. In public schools, guidelines focus on the child's present grade level in school, grade-level achievement in a subject area, and evidence of a discrepancy between the two. The student's overall intellectual ability is considered also. In Christian and private schools, the guidelines are often more flexible. In essence, students with problems go to whatever specialist may be available to help them. The label, although often needed to obtain services, isn't important; obtaining help in learning is important! The question should be: "Who in our school is best able to meet a particular student's needs?"

Meet Lance

Lance was a handsome, friendly sixth grader about whom the question

A taste of Blakberries

by Deris B. Smith

1 Jamie and his friend went to the Blackberries bush to try them they went to the apple tree

2 One day mrs. hogiser asked the kids see if they would want to

3 one day when mrs hoser ask the boy to picked the page of the grapse leaves and the were hiss around what a bear rest a gamee got seem

4 This chapter is when Jaime was picken and he stuck a stick in th tolle.

5 When Jamies frind went to the fenireel he look at him and ran outrid hisdad took his chead in his shouldl

6 This is when Jamie frend tryed to shranke in the garden

Lance's paper shows several characteristics of a child with a reading or learning disability: confusing words and letters and difficulty with spelling, grammar, and writing.

could be asked, "Is he LD or RD?" Actually, Lance could have been considered either or both, by any definition, in any school.

Lance was involved in a special education program in his Christian school. The class where he spent most of his time was not labeled. It was known simply as Mrs. Taylor's class. There were two classes that helped students with specific needs, one for intermediate grades and one for middle school. Mrs. Taylor's class was for middle school students. It was a class in which students spent varying amounts of time. More recently referred to as inclusive education, they joined students in the regular classes for some subjects during the day. Lance attended math and PE with the regular sixth grade class, while other students from Lance's class spent most of the school day in regular education.

Lance's learning problems encompassed all of the language arts areas. He read on a third grade level. His handwriting, spelling, and grammar were all significantly below grade level. Because of his reading and writing problems, content area subjects like science and social studies were difficult, too.

However, Lance did well in math computation. He could figure out problems accurately when they involved just the numbers. Story problems were difficult for him because of the reading involved. Lance also excelled in PE. He was an excellent athlete, agile and adept at basketball and soccer, a speed demon at track. He loved recess because he was always the captain of whatever team was being formed that day.

Diagnosing Lance's Learning Needs

Lance had been referred for psychoeducational testing in the early grades. A complete battery of tests was performed by his local public school district. The discrepancies between Lance's general ability and his achievement in reading and language were significant. His school noticed a widening gap, increasing year by year, between his current grade level and the grade level of his achievement in reading and language arts. Lance would have qualified as reading disabled or learning disabled in his local public school. In the Christian school which he attended, he qualified for Mrs. Taylor's room.

The psychoeducational evaluation had been performed by a school district psychologist who evaluated Lance's general intellectual ability (I.Q.), his achievement on standardized tests in various subject areas, and his emotional/social functioning. Lance was found to have average intellectual ability, grade-level achievement in the math areas, and achievement significantly below grade level in the reading and language arts areas. He was reported to be well adjusted, enjoying social activities and athletics.

Lance was somewhat concerned about his learning difficulties but seemed to have adopted the attitude, "Oh, well, what can I do?"

Mrs. Taylor had established a procedure for all students who were referred to her room. She reviewed all previous testing, teacher comments, report cards, and any other pertinent information in a student's file. She then established a list of possible strengths and areas of concern. She emphasized the word *possible*, because only direct interaction with a student could confirm each student's needs.

Mrs. Taylor did some informal testing with Lance. She had him read books at various levels and noted his reading behavior: rate of reading (silently and orally), ability to answer comprehension questions, ability to read single words and paragraphs, types of oral errors, and so on. She analyzed his strengths and areas of concern in reading and planned a program to meet his needs. She also had him do some writing in order to analyze his spelling, English grammar and usage, and handwriting. This was the kind of information which she needed to plan a language arts program for him. Test scores told her very little, but observing his reading and writing told her a great deal.

The next step in Mrs. Taylor's informal evaluation was to ask Lance to read a book independently and to answer some questions in writing. Mrs. Taylor chose a book at Lance's reading level, not his grade level, because she didn't want his reading difficulties to interfere with his writing. This assignment helped her evaluate the following: sentence structure, spelling, punctuation, capitalization, and handwriting. She was also looking for his accuracy in answering the questions. Could he answer them correctly? Could he answer them completely?

Lance's written response helped Mrs. Taylor decide on a plan of work for Lance. She was particularly eager to begin with his strengths. She smiled to herself, remembering that many teachers would simply mark the paper F and return it with the admonition, "Do it over. How can you hand in a paper like this?"

Mrs. Taylor had learned through her years of experience and her training that students who produced papers like Lance's were not just lazy or in a hurry. A paper like Lance's indicated real learning problems. But first, she reminded herself to look at the strengths.

Upon seeing Lance's paper, many teachers would throw up their hands and yell, "Help! Where do I begin?"

Mrs. Taylor was intrigued rather than frustrated. She saw the challenge in helping Lance. Which area should she begin with? Since she was planning a reading program, she decided to connect it with his writing needs.

She decided that the gist of Lance's writing problem was that he couldn't remember everything at once. He knew the answers, he knew about capital letters, and he knew about periods, but he seemed unable to accomplish all of them at the same time. Spelling concerned her more. His spelling seemed to show that he had difficulty visually remembering words. She also wondered how well he heard the differences among similar words. His handwriting indicated that he knew how to write the letters in cursive, but as he got frustrated or tired or the answers became difficult, his handwriting deteriorated.

Remediation

Mrs. Taylor saw many possibilities for helping Lance. The teaching strategies that she decided to follow can be used by students on their own, by tutors, and by parents who work with their children:

1. *To give Lance reading material similar in length and level of difficulty to the book he just completed.* He handled the reading well, and he needed other successful reading experiences.

2. *To give him four written questions instead of six.* Perhaps the assignment was too long and his writing "broke down."

3. *To have him say answers into a tape recorder.* This will enable him to concentrate on the content without worrying about the mechanics of capitalization, punctuation, sentence structure, and spelling.

4. *To have him listen to the tape recorder and transcribe onto paper what he has said.* This will give him the writing practice he needs after he has thought about the content. He won't have to think of what to write and also write it at the same time.

5. *To conduct a conference with Lance to discuss strengths and areas of concern,* including posing questions such as the following:

Capitalization: When do we capitalize words? Do you see any place in your first answer where you need a capital letter? Read the sentence aloud, and let's listen for the place where the sentence, or complete thought, ends and another begins.

Punctuation: Where do we put periods when writing? Do you see a place in your first answer where a period is needed?

Sentence Structure: Will you read number 2 aloud? How did you want that to end?

6. *To target one area on which to begin work, such as incorrectly spelled words.* Once a list of incorrectly spelled words is composed, the words can be presented to him one by one, to see if he can spell them. If not, the following sequence of visual, auditory, kinesthetic, tactile (VAKT) practice can be used:

a. The teacher writes the word in very large letters.

b. The student traces it and says it until he feels he knows it.

c. The student writes it three times.

d. The student writes it on an index card and files it in a word box.

e. The student reviews the words daily.

f. The student writes a sentence with the word on the back of the word card.

7. *To train Lance to go through the steps for learning spelling words in # 6 on his own for the purpose of developing self-regulation skills.* Since her time with Lance was limited, Mrs. Taylor trained him to do the visual, auditory, kinesthetic, and tactile technique in the previous step.

8. *To provide a checklist so he can search for errors on his own, providing he recognizes errors in spelling, grammar, punctuation, etc.* If he is unable to recognize errors, the teacher can mark each error and invite him to suggest what is wrong, thus "scaffolding" instruction to provide the amount of help he needs.

9. *To have him choose two answers to rewrite with the corrections.* Rewriting a whole sentence with corrections reinforces learning. Just patching up errors doesn't do as much. Choosing two sentences, rather than rewriting a whole piece, is realistic.

10. *To ask him to use his best handwriting in the rewriting task.* Since the size, shape, and space of the letters are quite good, he can be directed to improve his slant. Or he can word process if he has learned keyboarding which allows him to do his "writing" on the computer.

A frequent question today among parents, students, and teachers alike is when to introduce the computer and how much a student with problems like Lance's should use word processing. Should he do all work on the computer? How much attention should be given to handwriting? Would he use spell check effectively through the computer and would he remember it doesn't catch everything? These are valid considerations at a time when technology offers significant help to students like Lance.

Lance is one of many children whose reading disability is broader than just problems with the process of reading. An examination of his writing shows several areas, generally included under the language arts, in which he has difficulty. Analyzing his work provides an excellent source for planning remediation. By recognizing his strengths and tackling concerns, he can be helped. All children with learning problems have unique strengths and needs. The challenge is to identify both and to plan a program to meet their needs.

Adjusting to Changes and Challenges in Family Life

From Korea With Love:
A Personal Adoption Story

*"The anticipation of a child
is an exciting and frightening time."*
*"With the adoption of a foreign child ,
more uncertainty exists."*

"How can babies come from airplanes? I thought they came from mommies' tummies," mused my four-year-old daughter, Janine, as we discussed her new brother's arrival.

"Well, babies do come from mommies' tummies, and John did, too. But his mommy couldn't keep him, so he's coming here to be our baby," I explained.

"Can we keep him?" was her next question.

"Oh, yes, he'll be part of our family, just like you and Caroline," I answered.

"And Ellie," she added. Ellie was our dog.

"Will he look like this?" she continued, picking up a dark-skinned doll.

"Sort of, I think," was the best I could do for a reply.

"And will his hair turn white in the summer like ours?" she persisted.

"No, it will stay black." Finally she had asked an easy question.

"Well, I think I'll like him if he isn't mean like..." and she began to name some boys from the neighborhood.

"I think it's exciting, getting a baby from far away, don't you?" I asked.

"I guess so, yes, it's just—" she seemed to be searching for the right word, "different." I had to agree that she was right. It certainly was different from the way she and her sister entered our family and from the way most of her friends had entered theirs. While some of her friends had been adopted, she wouldn't have noticed because they usually had at least a passing resemblance to other family members. Janine's reactions to adopting a baby from another country were not unlike the attitudes of many of our adult acquaintances.

Why Adopt?

The pathway to parenthood has usually been a pretty direct route. Children came into the family by birth. When this route was blocked, adoption was considered as a way of establishing a family. For many years the majority of prospective parents seemed to follow a first-second sequence: first choice, birth children; second choice, adopted children. Recent trends suggest that many husbands and wives are taking an either/or approach. Their feelings run along these lines: "We would like to have children, and we would be happy with their arrival either by birth or by adoption. We are aware of the fact that many children need homes and, if it's God's will for us, we'll be happy to accept one or more of them into our family."

Seeking children in need of homes has resulted in a broader base of potential adoptees, including foreign children, biracial children, children with disabilities, and older children. This newer breed of adoptive parents looks beyond babies of their own race or nationality, seeking a child who needs them, rather than one who is most like them. These families face a sometimes difficult but tremendously exciting and gratifying set of challenges.

Our reasons for adopting a Korean child were partly humanitarian and partly selfish. We wanted a child who needed a home, and we also wanted a son. As an adopted child myself, I viewed adoption on a par with giving birth, a natural process by which God brought children into a family. Having two birth daughters already, we thought adoption would be a good way to expand our family.

The anticipation of a child is an exciting and frightening time. Once a child is conceived, parents await its arrival. With the adoption of a foreign child, more uncertainty exists. After the application, there are still many barriers which must be passed: a home study by a case worker from a social service agency, proof of orphan status from the overseas agency, certification of the child's health by an immigration official, proof of ability to financially support the child, governmental approval to bring an alien into the country, and a substantial fee to cover agency costs. As the red tape is gradually sliced away and the final goal is within reach, questions arise, "Will anything go wrong? Do we really want to go through with this? Wouldn't it have been simpler to have more birth children?"

A Scary Start

For our family, John's arrival was both expected and surprisingly sudden. Having just received word that he would come in six weeks, we received a call to meet him at the airport in four days. We scurried to get the nursery ready and to find some baby clothes left over from his sisters. We all drove to the airport wondering what our new son and brother would be like. Would he take to us? Would we like him? Would he miss his foster mother? What should we feed an 8-month old? We struggled to remember, to sort out our feelings, and to prepare ourselves. As we drove along, my husband asked how my labor pains were coming. I assured him that my rapidly beating heart told me the birth was imminent.

At 10:30 p.m. that night the 747 completed the last leg of its 27-hour flight from Seoul, Korea, and our son was delivered. Caroline and Janine wondered why their new brother was not only tan, which they expected, but also red. We soon realized that John was feverish, the result of a respiratory infection he had acquired on the trip. We took

Arden and Jack Post with Caroline and Janine as John arrives from Korea in 1972.

home a sick child and a prayer that things would go well. My parents, remembering my adoption, had come to the airport to take pictures. Later they told us that they had gone home and prayed that John hadn't arrived in this country only to die.

Back at home we got all three children ready for bed and dropped quickly into an exhausted sleep. It lasted 20 minutes. John had slept most of the 27 hours of the trip from Korea, and he was ready to get up. The infection made him fretful, and he began to cry loudly.

We tried to amuse him by setting him on the floor with some toys. He promptly fell over, and we remembered with some apprehension that both of our daughters had been able to sit up when they were his age. We put him on his tummy. He made no attempt to hold up his head. Now we were really worried. Quickly retrieving the baby book, we found that Caroline had been able to lift her head at 2 months. We tried to get a reaction from John to the few Korean words we had learned from the dictionary, but he didn't respond. Fear and panic set in. This wasn't turning out to be the joyful experience we had anticipated. Why had we imagined that adoption would be so wonderful?

With the new day came a visit to the doctor and some medicine which helped John get over the infection. The developmental lags remained, however, and only time would tell if John would catch up on motor skills and if his mental development would be normal.

From an inauspicious beginning, things did improve. Although John did not reach for toys or people—in fact, he reached for nothing except a bottle— his eyes searched everyone and everything. All of our neighbors came over to see the first foreign child on the block. The older boys decided that he should learn karate and, although the lessons had to be postponed, they continued to visit and entertain him.

Gradually, the developmental milestones which all anxious parents await, began to occur. After a few weeks he smiled at his own reflection in the mirror. He sat up alone at 10 months, began crawling at 11 months, and walked at 16 months. He spoke single words by his first birthday and short sentences when he was two.

While his development was gratifying, we faced a variety of reactions from people we encountered. Our church and our families had been supportive and loving, genuinely interested in John and generous in providing for him. Strangers, however, were another matter. Many people stared at us while others turned to look after we had passed by.

Young children asked some frank questions such as, "How come you have a Chinese baby?" I enjoyed these questions because I could answer them honestly. Young adults frequently were surprised when they learned that John belonged to us. Older people were another story. One day John and I were entering a store together. Two older women, worried that a two-year old would get his fingers caught in the door, exclaimed, "Little boy, where is your mother?" John looked at me, and I said, "Here I am." The ladies turned a deep scarlet, whispered, "Oh," and hurried off. Another episode occurred at the zoo. Jack was carrying John in a backpack while I trailed along behind. I noticed two people staring at my son and my husband. One said to the other, "Maybe his wife is Asian!"

Over the years people have often asked us how we feel about our foreign adoption experience. Our response is that it has been an exciting experience, a blessing from God, and a chance to grow together. We also have been asked if we have any advice for those just starting out in foreign or biracial adoption. There are three qualities of our relationships as a family which we have found to be essential to a successful experience.

- *You need a sense of humor.* Some people's words and attitudes may seem hurtful, insensitive, or insulting. However, we chose to see them as humorous. Each night at supper we enjoyed the events of the day, and the Korean-American connection found its way into our family chatter about interesting and amusing situations.

- *You also need to be open with one another.* We talked about differences from the day John arrived, not to make an issue of them, but to approach them openly. We also anticipated problems before they arose. For example, when we moved to a new location there was usually a rash of questions from children about John's origins. One of us would frequently accompany him and deflect questions if he became uncomfortable. Sometimes we would introduce ourselves along with our somewhat unique family.

• *This may sound trite, but we believe it's true: love conquers all.* Love in a family goes a long way, and we have found it possible to overcome minor trials and frustrations by our mutual support.

Our ABC's of Adoption

Since John's arrival we've been asked numerous times about how we decided to adopt and how we knew it was the right thing to do. The ABC's of adoption cover the steps we went through in deciding. They may be helpful to other families who are considering foreign or biracial adoption.

• *Ask God—Pray about it.* This is a necessary step in making any decision. Then let God lead, and look for small indications as to the direction that should be followed. The thunderbolt answer to a decision rarely occurs.

• *Be honest about your motives.* I once met a lady who wanted to adopt a "cute Korean child" because she missed her recently deceased father. This is not a good reason to adopt! Parents need to be honest with each other about the type of family they desire and the degree of difference within their family that they are willing to accept.

Audrey and John Post today with Samuel and Simon.

- *Consider your fears or hesitations.* We all have qualms when anticipating a child's arrival. For foreign or biracial adoption, parents often wonder how the child will be accepted, how he or she will feel in the family, what will happen with dating. These are normal concerns, and no one can give certain answers. We asked ourselves if we thought we could handle such issues and felt fairly confident that we could. We also agreed that we would seek professional help if it should be needed.

How to Decide

- *Discuss it with others in your circle of family and friends.* It's still your decision, but discussion may be very important to you if your relatives are uncomfortable with the idea or your friends are resistant to those of other races or nationalities.
- *Evaluate* your *present circumstances:* income, neighborhood, schools, mobility, church, and so on. Each family has its own set of circumstances to evaluate as to how a child will fit in. Since we moved frequently, we looked for schools in which other races were represented, locations in which other races were integrated, and churches in which other races were welcomed. This was not hard to accomplish, but we had to be ready to pursue it.

Even as we received the spirit of sonship and became children of God, many of us have received children into our families who are as much our sons and daughters as are our birth children. The wonder of adoption parallels in a small way the wonder of God's love and plan for us, his adopted children. From Asia, from North or South America, from Europe, from wherever God brings us children, they come for us to love and to raise to love him.

Remembering Buffy: Handling the Death of the Family Pet

"In short, she was a member of the family,
one who had few demands and loved unconditionally."

When our dog died after a brief illness, we realized what an important part of our family she had been. For ten years she had been a member of the family, one who had few demands and who loved us unconditionally.

Buffy, our cocker spaniel, was with our family almost ten years. She came on our daughter Janine's sixteenth birthday, promised in a moment of weakness long ago by Mom and Dad. As the years passed, we hoped she'd forget our rash promise. But children have long memories, especially about things they want, and the birthday prompted a renewed appeal for the long-awaited pet.

At a local kennel we saw several cocker spaniel puppies. Janine tried the "snuggle test," holding one of the cuddly puppies in her arms. The puppy passed the test, settling warmly against her and licking her hand.

"This is the one I want!" she exclaimed. "She's perfect!"

Janine Post has her graduation picture taken with Buffy.

"How about a poodle?" I asked. "Dad says they don't shed."

"You promised a cocker spaniel! That's what I've always wanted!" was her determined reply.

And so it came to be that at eight weeks of age and weighing five pounds, Buffy became the family pet. We followed the advice in the pet manual and let her sleep in Janine's room the first night to ease her fear of new surroundings. Buffy whimpered throughout the night. In the morning Janine was in tears. "I don't think I want her!" she cried. "I can't stay up every night!"

We assured her that Buffy would adjust. The next night the puppy slept downstairs in a box equipped with a warm blanket and a wind-up alarm clock. We'll never know how Buffy slept, but we slept well and were ready for an active day of puppy training the next morning.

In preparation for the arrival of a pet, my husband had said, "You children want a pet. Pets take a lot of care. Who's going to train it and feed it?"

"Mom!" replied all three offspring in unison. They all promised to help, of course. Exactly what that help would consist of was rather vague, but it seemed to include feeding and walking the dog occasionally. A few days after Buffy's arrival, Janine left for a young people's convention, and I was in charge of her pet.

A Part of the Family

The first year of a pet-in-residence included fun and frustration, time spent in playing but also in training and cleaning up. Caroline, Janine's older sister, decided that the dog needed to learn some tricks. The most novel one Caroline taught her was how to pray. When Caroline said, "Pray," Buffy would lie down on the floor and put her head on her paws. Of course, her "prayer" produced immediate results in the form of a treat.

John, our seventh grader, became the playmate—throwing a ball, tugging an old sock, and running around with Buffy for the active play time puppies need. He and his neighborhood friends amused her and were entertained by her.

Buffy was more than

John Post shows his love of Buffy, the family pet.

a cute, fun diversion. She was a source of comfort when someone was sad. She provided playful relaxation after tense days at work or school. She was a conversation piece, an aid to awkward teen dialogue. She was the one friend who came along when we moved to a new state. In short, she was a member of the family, one who had few demands and who loved unconditionally.

And so it went, adventure after adventure, as all three children grew up, attended college, and went off to lives of their own. Buffy officially became my dog when Janine got married and said, "Mom, my wedding present to you is Buffy."

As the years passed, we kept track of humorous canine events. One time Buffy got up on the table and ate a full bowl of candy hearts. Another time she encountered an unbaked loaf of bread rising in a pan and devoured the whole thing. She burped yeast and suffered a bloated belly for two days. Once she had a lunch of marshmallows after discovering how to open the lower kitchen cabinets.

One night we noticed that Buffy had a tender belly and her breathing was heavy, so we began asking what she could have eaten. The next day she was no better, so we visited the veterinarian. After some tests and x-rays, he diagnosed a serious, usually fatal, disease that strikes middle-aged dogs. He began an aggressive treatment of medication that had a small chance of success but that was worth trying for a couple of days. After an initially favorable response to the medication, Buffy began slipping. By the next day it was apparent that she was not responding and that she would not recover. We made the heart-rending decision to end her life. I held her while she slipped away.

We informed our children as soon as we knew the seriousness of Buffy's condition. This cushioned the news of her death, but they were still affected by it. Somehow the dog had been an inseparable part of the home, and they expected her to be there with greetings whenever they arrived.

Of all the family members, I was the most affected. Many people, young and old, students and teachers, offered sympathy and shared their experiences with pet loss. One father told me about the family dog dying in his arms as he and his young daughter carried it to the veterinarian. College students related how they still missed the family pet who was no longer home when they returned for vacations. Several teachers told me of their class's sorrow when the pet guinea pig or hamster died.

After a few days we got a new puppy, a buff-colored cocker spaniel named Sammy Jo. She diverted our attention, helped us deal with our grief, and filled the "pet place" in our hearts. She will never replace Buffy, but she has begun to create her own pet memories as she shares our daily lives.

As I write this essay, I see my husband walking outside in the yard with Sammy Jo, who is running, chasing squirrels, and basking in the sunshine. God gave us a wonderful world, and we believe that pets are a joyful part of it.

When A Pet Dies

1. *Recognize that pets play a significant part in the lives both children and adults.* It's natural to grieve their loss.

2. *Realize that people, even in the same family, may have had varying degrees of attachment to the pet.* Therefore, some may feel the loss more than others. Family talks about the pet and feelings about its death may be therapeutic.

3. *Avoid cliches that minimize the loss, such as, "Oh, it's only a dog."* To the child, adult, or the whole family, it was a significant being.

4. *Avoid saying "We put the pet to sleep,"* especially to young children who might not equate this expression with death. They may expect the pet to awaken or may come to fear sleep. Instead, say that the pet died.

5. *Be careful about differentiating among pets that you consider worthy of grief and those that you don't.* To a pet owner, a pet is a pet, whether a dog, a cat, a horse, a snake, a spider, or a parakeet.

6. *The hardest thing to discuss may be where the deceased pet is now.* We decided that Buffy simply ceased to exist. Some families have simply said that the pet is buried. Others have tried to answer questions about whether the pet is in heaven.

7. *Get a new pet if that seems right for the family.* Our veterinarian assured us that we weren't being disloyal to Buffy. Instead, Buffy had given us so much love and joy that we wanted another pet.

8. *Look for books in children's or young adult literature that deal with pets and loss.* A good book for young children is Judith Vorst's *The Tenth Good Thing about Barney* in which a child mourns the death of his cat and is helped through his grief by his parents and his friend.

Packing Up & Moving On: Families in Flux

"We had agreed to trust God to lead us into uncharted waters, but we weren't doing it. We were trying to handle the move all alone. . . . "

There have been attempts to characterize emotional stages that occur with loss, including denial, aggression, bargaining, depression, and acceptance (Kübler-Ross, 1969, 1991). While the stages originally referred to death and dying, these stages are also experienced in other situations involving loss—like the breakup of a relationship, alienation between friends, the loss of a job.

Not surprisingly, we see some of these same emotions when families move. Moving involves many losses as people, places, activities, and routines are left behind. However, moving is unique because it also may offer some advantages: a new house, a fresh start in school, a chance to see a new area of the country or world, and a good career opportunity for husband or wife. And people might be glad to leave some things behind: a house needing repair, a nosy neighbor, the bully down the street, or a less-than-ideal school or teacher.

Moving is a unique combination of pluses and minuses, and we found that a family can pass through some distinct stages.

- Finding Out: Fear may lead to Excitement
- Deciding: Excitement leads to Reality
- Facing the Decision: Reality may combine with Regret
- Working It Out: Regret can result in Action
- Moving at Last: Action is followed by Adjustment

Finding Out: Fear ➠ Excitement

"That was Mr. Henkel," said Janine. "Isn't he the real estate person?"

"I think so," responded her sister, Caroline. "What did he want?"

"He just asked for Mom or Dad. He said Dad called his office today. Why would Dad be calling him?"

"Oh, Mom probably wants to know what houses are selling for in the neighborhood. She always follows that in case we have to— to— to move." Then she continued in a more agitated tone, "Oh, no, not again. We just got here. It can't be!"

"I don't think that's it. Maybe they just want to move closer to the school." Janine's voice sounded more optimistic than she felt.

"You're right, and it would be great to live near school. No more 25-minute drives to basketball practice after supper and 25 minutes back late at night. Boy, would 1 love that!" Caroline exclaimed as she, too, tried to have a positive outlook. "Maybe we'll get to live near —"

Just then my husband, Jack, and I walked in. "Hey, y'all!" (We had really become Southerners!) "What's going on? You look excited about something. Let us in on it," said Jack with genuine interest.

"Mr. Henkel called. He said you called him today. Why? What's going on?" Janine could scarcely get the words out fast enough.

"Well," said Jack with a smile, "I've been offered a new job in Cincinnati. We didn't want to tell you until things looked more definite. I'm not sure I'm going to accept it."

The girls' initial fear turned to mounting excitement as the possibility became real. Suddenly they were giggling and asking lots of questions. Where would we live if we moved? What school would they go to? What kind of church would we attend? The questions tumbled out as their excitement grew.

"Wait a minute!" Jack exclaimed. "I said nothing is definite. It may be best that we stay right here."

"Do you want to go?" asked Caroline. She seemed to hit the nail on the head. If Jack wanted to go, the rest of us usually fell into line.

"You went to Cincinnati last week," Janine suddenly remembered. "Is that why?"

"Yes," said Jack, matter-of-factly. "I wanted to look around a bit."

"What's it like? Tell us!" the girls shouted together.

"Oh, the job, well, it looks challenging and —" Jack began.

"No, tell us about Cincinnati. Is it as nice as Atlanta? Did you visit a Christian school?" The girls knew Jack always did that before considering a move.

"Yes, I did, but wait a minute. I said nothing was decided. Let's give ourselves a little time to think and then we'll discuss it."

Increasingly, families are finding themselves in situations like the one described above. To move or not to move? It is a question requiring agonizing decisions. And many families face the decision repeatedly as they relocate from state to state or to foreign countries.

Deciding: Excitement ➠ Reality

Jack and I traveled to Cincinnati the next week. We visited the company offices briefly, but the job was the least of our concerns. We knew he would like it and was well suited for the challenge. But there were the many other factors we needed to consider: school, church, housing.

We have always believed that God provided direction when we faced what we had come to call "moving opportunities." That direction didn't come as a thunderbolt from the sky, a sudden answer that ended all speculation. Instead, it came in a number of small ways, as answers to the questions that were important to our family. Was there a Christian school with which we would feel comfortable? Was there a church consistent with our beliefs? Was there suitable housing close enough to school and church?

As each of these questions was answered affirmatively, our decision became clearer but not easier. We returned with lots of information for our family.

"Yes, we visited the Christian school. I think you will all fit in well there and like it," I replied in answer to their first questions. "There's only one small thing you might not like."

"Uh-oh," said Janine. "What's the small thing?"

"They have a rather strict dress code," I replied, trying to soften the blow.

"What do you mean by rather strict?" she asked.

"Girls must wear dresses or skirts."

"I'll die if I have to wear a dress or skirt every day!" Janine exclaimed. "Oh, Mother, how can you call that a minor matter?"

"Well, everything else about the school looks good. It's the same size as your school here, and it seems to be a fine Christian community."

"I'll never go to a school with a dress code!" Janine declared.

"Let me tell you the rest," I insisted, and we talked about the church and housing, both of which were agreeable.

"Are there lakes?" asked John, our fifth grader, who took great delight in fishing.

"They're not quite as close, but, yes, Ohio has lakes," Jack said patiently. "I do think it's God's will for us to go by the way he's shown us the answer to our questions about school, church, and housing."

We all gave our opinions. The three children agreed they would rather stay, but they would go if Dad wanted to. I felt the same way. Jack did want to, and our decision was made. Now excitement gave way to the reality of what was going to happen. Now came the harder part—trusting that God would work everything out.

Facing the Decision: Reality ➠ Regret

Once the decision was made to move, it became necessary for Jack to move before the rest of us.

In the middle of a rare Atlanta freeze, Jack left for Cincinnati, and the reality of our situation hit the children and me. That same night the humidifier on our attic heating unit froze, thawed, and sent a cascade of water pouring through the family room light fixture. Sound bizarre? It was. There seems to be something about moving that causes Murphy's Law: If something can go wrong, it will...and at the worst possible time! During our last *three* moves, we have had *three* hot water heaters go, always when Jack was gone.

Now reality set in for the children in very concrete ways. Caroline realized she would not be on the basketball team next year. Janine realized that her cheerleading days at DeKalb Christian Academy were over. Would she make the squad in a new school? Anxiety and reality went hand in hand.

At this stage the present situation—school, house, city, friends—always seems better than ever, and any undesirable aspects of the present situation seem benign. For example, the long ride to school didn't seem so bad anymore. Caroline was chosen homecoming princess for her tenth grade class. Fifth grade romances were blossoming, and John had a small group of girls who chased him around at basketball games to his delight. Janine's cheerleading squad was planning to attend a summer camp to get ready for the fall season. The homework grew lighter, and the teachers became nicer. Atlanta weather even became better than ever; spring came early and the cherry blossoms were gorgeous. In fact, it was so great living in Atlanta that we wondered why we had ever agreed to go.

Besides, we didn't like thinking about new challenges. Cheerleading and basketball were surely not as good in Cincinnati as they were at the present school. We'd never enjoy a house as much as we liked the present one. No groups of friends could ever equal those we now had. On it went, and the children were not alone. I had the best job in the world—resource teacher in a terrific school with outstanding administrators, colleagues, families, and students. The job was everything I'd ever wanted. Why had I agreed to go?

We wondered if Jack should get an apartment, come home when he could, and let the rest of us remain comfortably settled. But we decided that this course of action was not for us. Jack hated being away; he lost his appetite and a lot of weight.

We were reminded of Jesus' words about God's care of the birds of the air and the lilies of the field in Matthew 28. We truly fit the words, "... O you of little faith" Matt. 28:30b). We certainly were of little faith. We had agreed to trust God to lead us into uncharted waters, but we weren't doing it. We were trying to handle the move all alone, failing emotionally, and suffering greatly. But this stage of reality leading to regret paved the way for positive action to follow. We seized upon the words, "...do not worry... but seek first his Kingdom and his righteousness and all these things will be given to you as well" (Matt. 28:31a, 33).

Working It Out: Regret ⇒ Action

We have learned two things during our moving experiences. First, have a sense of humor or you'll suffocate. Second, this too shall pass.

Our house had been for sale for several weeks when we decided to take a quick trip to Disney World. One night at midnight after an exhausting day, the phone jarred us awake at our motel. Two offers had come through on the house simultaneously. A decision was needed; we presented a counter offer to the higher bidder and awaited a response. It came an hour later. We accepted it with certain conditions and awaited another response. By morning the house was sold, we hadn't slept, the weather was cold, and we were extremely crabby.

"Just think," we told the kids, "years from now you'll look back at this experience and laugh at how we spent one night of our spring vacation selling the house." They weren't convinced then, but now that's just what happens.

Probably every family that moves goes through the four Cs: chests, closets, cabinets, and cartons which have been stored in the basement since the last move. The fact of the matter is that taking inventory of the whole house from top to bottom is an extremely tedious, thankless, and time-consuming project.

"John and I cleaned out his chest today, and we decided to get rid of the *Letterbooks*," Jack announced one Saturday morning. He was referring to a set of 24 kindergarten workbooks designed for beginning reading. "He'll never use them again, and we've already 'enjoyed' them for five years," he added to tease me.

"But I might use them. Besides the scratch'n sniffs still work and we still look at them every once in a while!" I protested.

"Well, John says he doesn't want them, and I think he should decide!" Jack retorted.

"He only said that because he knows you're looking for stuff to get rid of! He probably figured you'd find something to throw out if he didn't!" I answered.

"They're in the trash if you want them," said Jack on his way out of the room. I retrieved the *Letterbooks* and hid them in a basement chest that would be moved intact. The workbooks remain there today; they do get used, and the scratch'n sniffs still work.

An endless assortment of such tasks faced us, but we consoled ourselves with the thought, "This too shall pass!" and it always did.

Moving at Last: Action ⇒ Adjustment

One month before leaving Atlanta, we moved out of our house and into the limbo of a furnished apartment. The place which had been our home for three years suddenly wasn't, and we had no new place, neither a house nor a city, to which we could attach ourselves yet.

The actual day of departure became etched in our memories, as it does for anyone who experiences long distance moves. This time we did not have crying children waving to crying neighborhood friends as the station wagon drove down the street for the last time. Instead, one friend of Caroline's took an early bus from the city to bid us farewell. As we drove to the bus stop that would return him home, the usual chatter about future plans occurred. He would come to Cincinnati next Christmas and bring a group of friends. Caroline and Janine would return to Atlanta during spring vacation. Words of comfort and hope, something to cling to, as that spark of regret was rekindled once again. Would these plans come to pass? Not likely, but they gave strength for the moment.

In Cincinnati we were immediately welcomed to the new neighborhood by two well-meaning ladies who stayed to visit for an hour. Eager to get on with the thousand tasks facing us and yet wanting an amiable start in a new neighborhood, we smiled at their exclamation, "We're so glad we caught you just as you arrived!" We wished they hadn't.

A new neighborhood in the summer can be great for young children who ride bikes, pull wagons, and often easily become absorbed into the daily play. For teenagers it can be another matter. Long days and nights of loneliness can set in. We were fortunate to begin attending a church which sponsored a youth group in the summer. Caroline, Janine, and even John, not yet in high school, were invited to attend. We had made our start.

The impending school year brought its own share of problems, however. Caroline was required to take two more years of history to meet Ohio requirements. Janine wistfully watched the cheerleaders practice even though she wasn't able to try out because try-outs were the previous spring. John entered a class that for the most part had been together since kindergarten and needed no newcomers.

Then came some of the hardest times a moving family can endure: the bedtime cries of sorrow for lost friends, fun, and familiar things. If only we hadn't moved!

It's at this point that trust in God became more crucial than ever. He had brought us this far; would he now help us the rest of the way? Our physical move was over, but our emotional one, with its day-to-day adjustments, had just begun.

God helped us again, not overnight and not by suddenly making things perfect, but by giving us three kinds of special grace: the grace to hang on while time allowed things to work out, the grace to work hard at making adjustments, and the grace to believe that his promises would come true. During a move problems can multiply. Superhuman strength sometimes is needed. Our family found that God provided it. As I wrote this article and asked my family for input, I found that some wounds are not completely healed. We moved again—this time from Cincinnati to Grand Rapids. It seems that we all leave a part of ourselves behind and take a part of our past locations with us each time. We did, however, come up with some suggestions for families who move.

Before Moving

1. *Ask God's will before deciding.* Let him lead you. As you consider the following suggestions, you will get answers which may be his means of helping you decide.

2. *Explore the features of a new community that will be important to your family—school, church, housing, recreation, or special needs.* If you can't travel there, contact a pastor who can give you names of people to get in touch with.

3. *Discuss the opportunity as a family.* List pros and cons. Give everyone a say in the matter even if parents make the final decision.

4. *Don't be influenced solely by a salary increase.* Moving costs are considerable, and it often takes a few years of the new salary to recoup added expenses.

5. *Commune with God.* Now that you're ready to make a decision, ask his help and then be prepared to exercise an enormous amount of trust during the next months.

As the Process Unfolds

1. *Be realistic.* You might not get the dream house you envisioned when you agreed to move. The country setting convenient to the city may not exist, or your favorite house may be too expensive. Realistic expectations will prevent grief during house hunting.

2. *Develop a list of priorities.* Is it important to be near school, church, work? You may not get all three. Is a family room, an extra bathroom, or a porch most important? A compromise will likely be necessary.

3. *Adopt a sense of humor.* You'll need it! Remember Murphy's Law. We now expect our hot water heater to break down as soon as the house goes up for sale.

4. *Be sensitive to children's reactions as events unfold.* Be available to answer questions, chat, and show concern for their needs and fears.

5. *Trust in God's promise to lead you through the frustrations and work all things to your good.*

6. *Remember that this too shall pass.*

After the Move

1. *Get acquainted with people.* Church is the best place to start. Attend services and special events. Go to the family night supper. Get involved in

projects. Invite a family over; they may not ask you first.

2. *Find out what the new location has to offer.* Visit the attractions of the area: a local recreation area, museums, shopping malls, sports events, even if it means postponing painting and wallpapering. These activities bind the family together when togetherness is most needed and provide relief from the trauma of settling in.

3. *Expect some sorrow and regret.* Adjustments take time, and the family may shed tears together with one member who is having a hard time. Then look for some positive action to overcome problems.

4. *Adopt a positive outlook and have faith.* Find the good things to build upon, and allow time in a new location to work in your favor.

5. *Don't work day and night.* The initial time in a new place is when the family needs both parents the most. Resist the temptation to put a new job ahead of all else.

6. *Moms often have the most difficult task.* In some cases, the kids are at school and Dad is at work while Mom looks at having to start from scratch: finding a new job, joining a new group, making new acquaintances, and navigating unfamiliar streets. Or it may be that the family has moved because of Mom's career opportunity. In this case, it's Dad who may need to start over. In either case, don't give in to depression. Make yourself get going. Make the first move. It's to the whole family's benefit!

Here Comes
Summer!

*"All around us are inexpensive materials
and valuable junk which can be used
for summer fun and creative play."*

Summer comes as a mixed blessing. There's relief from the hectic pace of the school year but, with the children constantly around, trying to find ways to keep them occupied can be difficult. Advice for what to do with the

long summer hours is easy to come by, but it's not always easy to follow. For example, everyone likes vacation trips, but who can afford to take a trip for the entire summer? Teachers urge parents to keep reinforcing academic skills—particularly reading—when the kids are out of school, but have you ever tried to get a reluctant reader to read a book while her friends are playing just outside the room where she is sitting? Other experts suggest that parents should encourage children to explore new games and play with new toys. But there's a limit to how many games and toys can be

Children care for a neighbor's pet as a summertime activity. They walk the dog and feed it while its owners are on vacation.

bought, let alone stored in the house.

What to do? Here are several suggestions for how to make this summer an enjoyable but also rewarding time for your family.

Family Trips

In many families, vacations have come to mean trips to a Disney attraction or travels across the country. Other families still enjoy "low-budget" vacations like camping or visiting relatives. However, the problems with vacations are that not all families can afford them, nor do they last a whole summer. But nearly every family can enjoy short, close-to-home trips. These outings can be used as a way to encourage children to observe new sights closely. Discussing the experiences with children, before, during, and after the outing, enriches their store of knowledge. Helping them sort out their observations and conclusions develops thinking skills. There are several types of short excursions that can be appropriate for children of various ages.

1. *Backyards, local fields, nature centers.* Notice the plants, insects, and changes from spring to summer and again as fall approaches. Bring along a book that identifies plants and insects.

2. *Local, state, or national parks.* Parks are excellent places in which to observe people, animals, and nature, as well as play equipment and picnic areas.

3. *Museums.* Many communities have several types of museums avail-

able, featuring art, history, science, technology, or nature. Let your children help choose the one to visit. Children's museums exist in many cities as do specialty museums featuring toys, sports, cars, or railroad memorabilia. Call ahead to find out if special exhibits are on display or if there are displays geared for different ages.

4. *Local recreation programs.* In addition to organizing neighborhood playground activities, these programs often sponsor trips to nearby zoos and parks.

5. *Fairs.* A state or county fair can be as exciting today as it was when grandparents were growing up. Later, children may talk about sounds and smells, animals, rides, and games. Many fairs continue to have 4-H exhibits that supply an educational experience as well as the typical fair activities like rides and food booths.

6. *Fast food restaurants.* These are always a favorite. Children can read the menu, figure out the cost of the meal, compare prices, discuss nutrition, or just spend the time enjoying Mom or Dad's company. While few of us want to make fast food a staple of our diets, it can be a real treat for children.

7. *Shopping centers.* Children with birthday money or allowances will enjoy the time to look for items to purchase. It's also useful to help children learn how far a few dollars go. They can compare quality and prices from store to store. Teenagers appreciate doing school shopping on their own and beginning it early, since fall displays in stores appear early in the summer.

8. *Grocery store.* Children can help make the grocery list, look for special items featured in the store's advertisement, consider the origins and ingredients of foods, and help prepare meals. Some teenagers may do the family shopping voluntarily, or working parents might consider asking teenagers to take turns at the shopping.

9. *Airports.* Children can read the signs, and the arrival/departure schedules, locate the gates, observe the employees, security measures, planes, and passengers, or plan an imaginary trip.

10. *Libraries.* Allow children to browse. You may have to encourage teens to come along, but once they are in the library they will probably find something of interest. Ask the librarian or children's librarian for recommendations of new or exceptional books. Ask about summer reading clubs, films, story hours, or other activities the library sponsors.

11. *Neighbors.* Encourage children to offer some time to help neighbors: water plants, care for pets, retrieve mail and newspapers. Helping others can be one of the most rewarding summer activities, and may even earn a little spending money.

Summer Reading

On previous pages the article, "Boosting Reading at Home," provided ideas for parent-child interaction in reading. The suggestions in that article are valuable for any time of the year, but summertime poses some special challenges. The International Reading Association publishes an annual pamphlet called "Summer Reading is Important." You can obtain a free copy by sending a stamped, self-addressed envelope to the Association's headquarters, P.O. Box 8139, Newark, Delaware 19711. Many of the tips below come from the IRA's annual booklets:

1. *Link reading to outdoor activities and sports.* Biking, swimming, boating, camping, soccer, baseball, basketball, football—the list of summer activities is almost endless. Books, magazines, and newspaper articles on your child's favorite activities may interest him or her. Of special interest may be stories of sports heroes or events, animal adventures, nature books, popular book series, and award-winning books.

Swimming is a favorite summer activity.

2. *Vacation trips.* Let children read about where you're going and help prepare for the trip. They may also read the map and road signs to give directions and find interesting information in brochures and postcards. Wherever you go, there are a lot of words and numbers.

3. *Household chores.* Anything Mom, Dad, older brother or sister do around the house can be a source of fun, participation, and learning for younger children: following directions for food preparation, cleaning, laundry, items to build, or even homemade directions for setting the table and other chores. All of these provide useful reading opportunities for youngsters.

4. *Writing.* It's important to reinforce the connection between reading and writing. The list of possibilities for summer writing is a long one: overdue notes to grandparents; diaries with a line, a paragraph, or a page a day; a summer story with illustrations to post on the refrigerator; a scrapbook of summer activities with captions; lists of things to do or items to buy; and many others.

5. *Connecting with TV.* Find books with themes or characters that relate to favorite shows. Read the TV schedule; look for programs based on books or stories; read about TV personalities in magazines or the newspaper; but

limit the endless TV viewing that can occur in the summer.

6. *Telephoning.* A young child may find it exciting to learn how to use the telephone book—locating names, reading across the row, using the yellow pages, finding area codes and rates.

7. *Computer games and CD-ROMs.* Many exciting, educational adventures await children. Broderbund's Talking Storybooks encourage interaction and feature popular series like the Arthur books by Marc Brown and the Little Critter series by Mercer Mayer. For older children following the Oregon Trail with a CD-ROM sparks interest in reading and geography.

Creative Play

Young children enjoy making things: cutting, pasting, drawing, coloring, painting, and sculpting. Here are a few items that are found in or easily acquired by most households: magazines, newspapers, catalogs, paper, paper bags, pencils, paintbrushes, finger paint, yarn, thread, ribbon, string, boxes, bottles, egg cartons, toothpicks, popsicle sticks, straws, play dough mixtures, buttons, spools, plastic bottle tops, plastic margarine containers, macaroni, alphabet noodles, old wallpaper books, scraps of material and trim, acorns, pine cones, twigs, and rocks.

Given an assortment of items, children enjoy making their own creations. For the reluctant beginner, here are a few ideas. Some may require a little assistance.

1. *Puzzles.* Cut an interesting picture from a magazine, paste it on sturdy cardboard, and cut it into various shapes to make a new puzzle.

2. *Puppets.* To make a paper bag puppet, use the folded bottom of the bag as the head and face. Glue on yarn for hair and eyebrows, buttons for eyes. Make other features with crayons, markers, or cut paper. Old socks make good puppets too.

3. *Paper art.* Cut all kinds of shapes from newspaper or colored construction paper. Rectangles and squares make good buildings; circles and ovals can become trees and flowers. Children can let their imaginations run wild!

4. *Pencil holder and jewelry box.* Dry macaroni (preferably the shell type) can be dipped in water which has had food coloring added. Dry out the macaroni noodles on wax paper and glue them on an orange juice can that has been covered with paper towel. You've got a pencil holder which may be varnished or covered with shellac. Or, glue white noodles of many shapes onto a box with a hinged lid. Spray with gold paint for a jewelry box.

5. *Play dough.* Here is the easy recipe: Mix together 1-1/4 cups flour, 1/2 cup salt, 1 cup boiling water, 1-1/2 tablespoons corn oil, and 1/2 tablespoon alum powder (available from pharmacy). Food coloring can be added. Keep the dough in the refrigerator when it's not being used and allow it to soften at room temperature for ease of manipulation.

Arden Post and granddaughter, Courtney Cone, participate in a creative, summertime activity.

6. *Flowers.* Egg cartons make easy flowers. Simply cut them apart into separate sections, trim each section to form any shape, and put a hole in the bottom of each section with a straw through it for a stem.

7. *String art.* Put a small dab of paint in the middle of a piece of construction paper. Let each child twirl a string across the paper to create a design. An object on the end of the string adds an interesting pattern. A related activity is "marble madness." Put a sheet of paper in a small rectangular container like a dish pan or cake pan. Add some drops of paint to the center. Put a marble in the center and tip the container slightly front to back and side to side.

8. *Greeting cards.* Old wallpaper books provide many different kinds of paper that can be cut into colorful greeting cards. Pasting construction paper inside will provide a good space for writing the message.

9. *Rock art.* Collect rocks in a variety of sizes and shapes. Paint them to look like insects (ladybugs are a favorite) or glue them together to form animals.

10. *Animal banks.* Small, plastic margarine containers can be turned upside down with the lid on the bottom. Add a slot for the coins, and decorate the bank with fabric or buttons. Fake fur is a favorite!

All around us are inexpensive materials and valuable junk which can be used for summer fun and creative play. These activities are also great for rainy days or times when kids are getting over illnesses.

Happy summer and have fun!

Christmas:
'Tis the Season to be Jolly?

"Why is it, then, that many people experience a feeling of sorrow at this time of year?"

Christmas is coming! Television and radio blare the news: "Only 20 more shopping days!" Bright lights and seasonal decorations appear throughout towns, in stores, and on homes. Christmas carols are sung enthusiastically by renowned choirs, popular singers, and local carolers. Good times, good food, and good fun abound at open houses, company parties, and church socials. Children and teachers prepare for Christmas programs and class parties. Churches also proclaim the good news—Christ is born, although these simple words may appear almost anticlimactic in the midst of the glitter and grandeur of the season. Everyone seems caught up in the fun and festivity which gain momentum as December 25 approaches.

Why is it, then, that many people experience a feeling of sorrow at this time of year, ranging from a twinge of sadness upon hearing familiar Christmas carols to a deepening melancholy as the season unfolds? What are the causes of the Christmastime blues—not the typical letdown after the season ends, but the feeling of sadness in the midst of such gaiety in December? Do only a few people experience this kind of sadness, or do many suffer through the year's happiest season?

Dr. Daniel J. David, in an article published in *The Journal of Family Practice,* identifies three general types of stress that can contribute to holiday depression. Socioeconomic stress hits those who are unemployed or who have low incomes; it can also strike at those who have good jobs but who feel the pinch of extremely tight budgets and the pressure of gift buying or other expenses. Psychological stresses can afflict those who are far away from family or friends or those who mourn the death of a relative. A heightened sense of one's own mortality or unresolved psychological conflicts can also be related to this type of stress. Biological stresses are brought on by different patterns of eating, drinking, or sleeping during the holiday season.

Sharing Christmas with loved ones is our greatest joy... but when we lose them, the season can bring sadness.

Over the past few years I've spoken with students in education courses at various colleges to find out their experiences with a feeling of melancholy in December. A recurring theme in many of their comments was "All around me was happiness, and people seemed to tell me that I must be happy too. Yet something in my life made this impossible. The very fact that such joy existed made me feel worse, resentful that I couldn't experience it."

For example, Tom recalled his childhood: "Everywhere I turned there were advertisements for Christmas gifts. My friends made long lists and were sure to get at least half of their requests, but my parents could barely afford one present for each of us. I know that my parents had that same 'down' feeling that we kids had each holiday season."

Anne's parents' divorce became final one month before Christmas: "Christmas that year reminded us of times when we had been a family. Now we were only a partial family. Christmas is a family day, but we didn't really have a family anymore!"

Sue remembered the times when all the relatives came for Christmas supper: "We had such a clan and it was hectic, but great fun, to be together. Now my husband and I and our children live far from relatives. We spend Christmas alone—just the four of us--with no relatives we can visit or with whom we can exchange gifts. Christmas for us is lonely, it reminds us of good times back home. I always take a supply of Kleenex to church on Christmas Eve. I think I do more crying in December than in all of the other months combined!"

Just after Jim entered fourth grade, his father died. Jim recalled, "In the fall it was rough enough, but when December came, the world caved in on me. My teacher and my classmates tried so hard to make me feel good.

Miss Brown made me her special helper. When we drew names for a small gift exchange, I got a better gift than anyone else because my silent partner felt sorry for me. Really, all the fun and festivity made things worse. I just needed someone to say, 'I know how you feel. Go ahead and cry. You don't have to be happy!'"

Other students had memories of similar circumstances that led to sadness at what should have been the happiest time of the year. Amy remembered the frustration of trying to pick out Christmas gifts on a limited budget, causing her to want to give up in despair. Karen remembered the round of activities that engulfed her upon returning home from college, when all she wanted to do was catch up on sleep. Tim remembered the phone calls from friends the day after Christmas, wanting to compare gifts. Since he usually received the least, the calls left him depressed and irritable. On they went, the causes of Christmastime blues. They ranged from the once-in-a-lifetime catastrophes to the predictable, annual occurrences that evoked the same unhappy feelings each year.

What went through my mind as I heard these stories and saw the pain reflected in the eyes of those who told them was that many of us miss the whole point of Christmas, completely avoid the true issue, and ignore the real reason for celebration. *Christ was born!* The magnitude of this event transcends earthly concerns and present sorrows. In fact, the seasonal reminder of Christ's birth should bring love, joy, and peace in the midst of earthly sorrow, disappointment, and loneliness. Why weren't we focusing on it?

I decided to interview older people, wondering if the younger generation was unique in paying attention to peripheral matters while overlooking the crux of the season. But the answers were similar. Older people missed departed relatives, children living far away, younger days with good health, more prosperous times, and a host of other situations when life was better. Their regret was real, and their sadness was justified. However, several were convinced that they couldn't possibly enjoy Christmas in view of their circumstances. Again, I wondered about the focus of the event: *Christ is born!* Because of this we have comfort readily available for this life, and we should have joy transcending the present moment.

Christ came that we may have life and have it more abundantly, not necessarily in the tangible aspects of family, friends, funds, and festivity, but in the everlasting promise of earthly care and heavenly glory. Does this mean that no sorrow is permitted at Christmas despite a broken marriage, a deceased relative, poverty, or loneliness? Of course not, but the focus of Christmas ought to be on what Christmas *really is,* not or what it *presently isn't* in terms of the world's standards. Here are some suggestions which are appropriate for all of us as Christians: parents, teachers, and students.

1. *Focus on the Christ in Christmas.* Read the Christmas story and the

These children help others experience Christ in Christmas by participating in a live nativity on a farm in Zeeland, Michigan.

Easter story, and discuss the implications they have for us.

2. *Apply the Christ in Christmas to personal situations.* If a loved one has died in the Lord, consider the glory he or she is now experiencing. Remember Christ's promise to believers to be with us always. If family problems exist, take courage from God's promise to be our refuge and strength. Instead of regretting the kind of Christmas gifts you can't buy, rejoice in the greatest gift—God's Son.

3. *Be sensitive to people who have experienced a loss that makes the holidays particularly difficult.* Cry with them; don't try to jolly them out of their sorrow by emphasizing festivity. Look with the sorrowing to Christ, the source of joy in the midst of sorrow. Recall Christ's promise to be with us always, and seek to be his agent of reconciliation in a broken world.

4. *Don't allow yourself to be caught* up *in the irrelevancies of Christmas.* Don't allow presents and parties to overshadow Christ's birth.

5. *Find someone for whom you can make Christmas a joyous season.* In this way you will be giving of yourself as God gave his Son for us. You will also experience the real joy of Christmas and remove the focus from yourself.

We can do much to set the stage for what Christmas means to our children. We can show them that we are caught up in the trappings of the season, for which worldly wealth and happiness are important. Or we can show them that the real joy of the season comes from celebrating Christ's birth and its implications for our lives. Let's choose wisely.

A Psalm for Christmas Eve *by Joseph Bayly*

Praise God for Christmas.
Praise Him for the Incarnation
for Word made flesh.
I will not sing
of shepherds watching flocks
on frosty night
or angel choristers.
I will not sing
of stable bare in Bethlehem
or lowing oxen
wise men
trailing distant star
with gold and frankincense and myrrh.
Tonight I will sing
praise to the Father
who stood on heaven's threshold
and said farewell to His Son
as He stepped across the stars
to Bethlehem
and Jerusalem.
And I will sing
praise to the infinite eternal Son
who became most finite
a Baby
who would one day be executed
for my crimes.
Praise Him in the heavens.
Praise Him in the stable.
Praise Him in my heart.

The late Joseph Bayly was president of David C. Cook Publishing Company at the time of his death earlier this year. Bayly was a widely published author whose writings often reflect the comfort and peace to be found in God's sovereignty in the midst of sorrow. This poem is from Psalms of My Life, *copyright 1972, Tyndale House. © 2000 Victor Books. Reprinted by permission.*

Letting Go:
A Child Leaves for College

"It may be a painful process—letting go
of the close parent-child relationship of youth and entering
into a parent-adult relationship in the college years."

An anxious yet awesome moment has arrived. Tomorrow we bring our oldest child to college. In a way, we have been preparing for this day ever since she was born; it has been a gradual process of letting go. Birth itself was a physical separation between mother and child. In the toddler years, the words "all by myself" indicated when she could walk alone, put on a shirt, zip a zipper, or do any of the countless tasks a child learns to do without help from Mom or Dad. Then came kindergarten when she proudly entered the school bus for the first time and waved good-bye. I turned away and shed some tears, happy that she had come so far, yet sad that she was moving into a world away from me.

Each year brought new moves toward separation and independence. We lived through the first sleepover at someone's house, the first over-night

High school graduation is a milestone that families celebrate. . . but then we need to
"let go" of our children as they head for college.

trip with a church group, and the ultimate—a week away at camp.

In high school there were more opportunities to be away. Traveling with a school sports team to other cities, attending a church-sponsored convention in another state, and finally, visiting prospective colleges—all nudged us toward a longer separation.

Leaving for College

Shopping, organizing, packing—finally the preparations were finished, leaving only the final farewells to friends. The night before leaving we were all restless, anticipating and dreading the morning's arrival when we would drive our daughter to college, a 10-hour trip across three states.

The trip began with excited chatter about new places, new people, and new opportunities while underneath there festered an anxious uncertainty. She wondered, "Will I like it there? Will I make friends? Can I handle the school work?" We wondered, "Will she come home again? Will she still need us? Will she meet someone, marry, and stay there forever?"

A variety of stories are told by parents about their children's arrival at college. Many parents report being left with the suitcases while their son or daughter goes off searching for acquaintances. Some say that the young person seems to disown them upon arrival, not wanting to be seen in the care of Mom or Dad. A few families have experienced tearful children for whom the new college scene is bewildering and unsettling. They are ready to turn around and head for home, and the parents don't quite know what to do! While the experiences vary we share much in common: children and parents are embarking on the biggest separation of their lives thus far, and the anxiety this produces manifests itself in different ways.

Our experience was a nightmare, but it will show how parents and child can survive one of the worst possible scenarios. We arrived in Nashville, Tennessee, knowing no one. Our daughter, Caroline, was entering a graduate program in nursing at Vanderbilt University, so we had actually been through a letting-go process once before. We should have been used to it, but this experience was different. Missing were the relatives who greeted us when we brought her to college four years earlier. Missing were friends whom she already knew when she arrived at college. Missing, too, was a clean dorm room with some potential for hominess. Instead we walked into a three-room, scantily furnished apartment. A linoleum floor with tiles missing, a rusty refrigerator with a shoebox-size freezer, and a chipped table created a very depressing first impression. Could we actually leave her here?

Caroline went with us to the motel where we'd made reservations for the night. What to do now? Did she want to forget the whole thing and come home with us? No. She'd made her decision, and she'd stick it out. Besides, she predicted that when her roommate arrived, they would fix up the apartment and things would improve. I predicted (rather hopefully) that in one month she'd be happily settled and would look back upon her opening days with amusement. We said good-bye through tears. Mine flowed openly while she stifled hers, assuring us she'd be fine. Dad gave her his longest hug ever while fighting the tears which he didn't want to show.

Adjustments for Students and Parents

It often takes a month for a new student to adjust to the college scene. But in this case, one month turned into two, two became three, and still she was unhappy, citing a list of regrets. The roommate missed a boy friend back home and left. There seemed to be few young people with similar interests at the college, and the local church had few college students attending at that time. The struggle went on.

On her first trip home two months into the semester, Caroline was filled with regret when it came time to return, but she was still determined to stick it out. It was during the next trip home that we saw a change. She enjoyed being home but was ready to return to college. At Christmas she announced that things were working out. She enjoyed her program, she had made some friends, and she was generally content. We sighed in relief and thanked God.

Our relief that the adjustment was progressing well soon gave way to another kind of anxiety. Would she adjust so well and like it so much that she would continue to live ten hours away after graduation? Worse yet, would she move even farther away after completing her program?

We experienced many ambivalent feelings at this time: relief that she had settled in, fear that she would not return, happiness that she was happy, sadness that she was far away.

Letting go of children as they enter college is traumatic for parents and children. The young person is struggling with identity, independence, and intimacy. In forging an identity the student wonders, "Who am I, especially in this new situation? Will I change? What is the 'me' I want to project?" In seeking independence, the young person wonders, "How will I handle my new freedom? What would I like to do that I haven't been able to do at home? What will it be like being on my own?" And in matters of intimacy, the student wonders, "With whom will I develop friendships? What kinds of girls and guys do I want to hang out with? Who will I date?"

Parents struggle with these issues, too, in a somewhat different way. "How will we like the changes in our child, and how will we relate to the new identity that is sure to emerge through maturity and experience? Can we handle our child's growing independence? Will we approve of the friendships she establishes?" Parents also face similar issues for themselves: "What is our identity now that our child is gone? How will we react to our new

Moving into the college dorm is exciting, but bittersweet for parents—less so for students.

independence?"

Parents who are about to take a son or daughter to college often ask if there is any way to ease the trauma. Are there any principles to help in this transitional period? Some pointers may help from the experiences of those who've survived and even thrived in the letting-go process.

Advice to Parents on Letting Go

1. Openly discuss your feelings about the pending separation. You can express pride in your child's accomplishments and regrets at her leaving. This creates a climate where she, too, feels free to discuss her feelings. Somehow, facing them head on and getting them out in the open makes everyone feel better and acknowledges that there are adjustments to be made.

2. Allow plenty of preparation time for shopping, packing, and moving. Try to be ready several days ahead of departure so there is time for last-minute purchases or a search for missing items. Last-minute pressures increase everyone's anxiety level!

Some parents wonder who should do the packing. It varies. In general a parent shouldn't take over the task but should stand by, offer assistance, and then do what is asked. This posture shows concern and interest while permitting independence.

3. Settle the issue of finances. Every one involved should be clear about who will pay for what, especially the incidentals like toothpaste, Friday night pizza, additional clothing purchases, entertainment, and trips home.

While the major issues of tuition and room and board are settled by the time a child leaves, smaller financial matters often are not settled, potentially causing stress and strain from a distance. Contingency funds, set up before departure, are worthwhile.

4. *Communication begins at home.* Talk openly about how you'll keep in touch. Will you call her? May she call you collect? Will you provide a calling card? Will you write to each other? How about e-mail?

I have noticed resentment among students whose parents set down strict guidelines such as, "Call us every Sunday afternoon," or "We expect one letter a week." It is more helpful for parents to give the young person some stamped self-addressed envelopes or postcards and ask that he or she drop a line frequently. Better yet, take advantage of the ease of e-mail.

Children appreciate an invitation to call home at any time. While this can cause some horrendous long-distance bills, such calls usually diminish after a month or two. Calls to the child to say, "Hi, how are you?" are appreciated if they don't turn into "20 questions" or "20 suggestions" on what to do.

5. *Talk about academic expectations.* This is a difficult topic because some young adults will work extremely hard to get A's and need to be told to relax and enjoy college life. Other students may be high on the enjoyment end of the continuum and need firm guidelines about the kind of grades that are expected. It is best for each family to judge its handling of grade expectations.

Parents should remember that grades often drop from high school to college, and midsemester freshman grades are frequently low. Low midsemester grades sometimes come as a surprise to freshmen. This can be a sobering experience to which many students respond with an effort at improvement. Most parents expect good effort from their children and know them well enough to judge whether that effort has been made.

6. *Values should be ingrained by now.* A frequent occurrence in many families is "The Reminder Chat." It starts off with parents reviewing their teachings of the last eighteen years as well as a summary of their moral and ethical values. It goes something like this: "You know that your mother and I don't approve of drinking. We hear that there are parties at college with drinking, and we expect you to stay away from them."

The problem is that there is no way the parent can maintain control of what the child does without literally sitting outside the dormitory. It is far better for parents to acknowledge the freedom and temptations and then to cite reasons for concern. By the time a young person graduates from high school, most values have been internalized, *taught* but also *caught,* and are unlikely to change with last-minute sermons. College students may question those values and experiment with different values. But in most cases, a firm foundation of values becomes an anchor with which to weather the storms and temptations of college life.

7. *Recognize the young person as a decision maker.* Who will make major decisions in the student's life during the college years? Will he go to summer school or work? Will she work at a camp or return to a summer job at home?

This is another thorny issue without an easy answer, and compromise is often required. Once the issue of finances is settled, the student knows the amount of money she will need to raise. The choice should be hers as to how she can meet that responsibility.

8. *College students must be allowed to make their own career choices.* Parents can advise and inform from their knowledge and experience, but it is the young adult who has to live with the career.

Sometimes students have difficulty deciding on a career. They seem to hop from one major to another and prolong college by one or two years as they try to make up their minds. My advice to such students is to get a general liberal arts degree, experiment with some career possibilities, and later return to college if more education is needed for a specific career.

There is another word of caution here. Parents can help their children tremendously by empathizing with the myriad choices which face young people today. They can show interest by talking through career options. They can also ease up on the pressure while still affirming the extent of time—for example, four years—that they will support the young person's studies. However, it is increasingly common for students to spend a fifth year in college. There is value in an extra year to mature and firm up vocational plans.

9. *Prepare yourself for changing relationships with your child.* She may vary from extremely dependent to independent. During the freshman year you may receive calls about minor issues. By the sophomore year you may learn about a change of major when she casually mentions it. Independence will grow, and this is good. It will be evident during the first visit home when your rules are challenged and you are confronted with an "almost adult."

10. *Find yourself something new to do.* There will be a vacuum created by a child's departure. Parents who are involved daily in a career may escape this feeling of emptiness, especially during working hours. Parents who are at home much of the day often feel the emptiness more. This is a good time to take on something new.

Some parents have taken steps to mark this new point in their lives and to relieve the emptiness of a departing child: taking a college course themselves, becoming involved in a church group, volunteering in a community project, joining a health club, visiting the elderly, returning to work, or changing a job with better opportunities. The point is that parents who actually seek to find themselves after a child leaves for college are better able to deal with the child's departure and better able to let the child go.

It may be a painful process—letting go of the close parent-child relationship of youth and entering into a parent-adult child relationship in the college years. But if this letting go never occurs—if parent and child continue to be mutually dependent—wouldn't the situation be much worse?

The College Experience: What If?

- If the young person calls home desperately homesick and wants to return, it may be wise to suggest that she stick it out at least one semester. Even the most homesick young person has usually adjusted by that time, but if things don't work out, a different course of action can be followed later. Contacting someone at the college who can help or a friend or relative in the area may be a good idea.
- If the child wants to come home for a visit, it may be wise to wait a month or so. The familiarity of home and friends can be a lure that keeps the student from adjusting. A homesick young person who visits home too soon may have a harder time adjusting.
- If the student develops a desperate need for money, it might be wise to

Graduating from college is often the stepping stone to further education. These future nurses, receiving their B.S.N. degrees, will be involved in lifelong learning.

loan the money and during the next visit home agree about how repayment will be made and how to handle future emergencies.

- If the student calls home with a serious complaint about the college, talk to someone at the college who can help you and her. The student affairs division is a good place to start. Listen to both sides of the story, ask for information, then work to solve the problem together.
- If the student calls home with a list of woes, empathize, offer advice if it seems appropriate, then say you'll call back in a day or two. Often you will find a happier young person, and you will feel better. Ups and downs are a common college experience.
- If you feel terribly lonely, call your child or go for a visit, but be careful not to let your feelings rub off on her, making her adjustment harder. Letting go is necessary for both of you.
- If possible, visit your child at college. Parents weekends are specifically designed for this, but any occasion will do. It is a treat for students to show parents around and be taken out to eat. Caution: Do not enter the student's dorm room and begin to clean it up or give her a list of instructions. You will find a more grown-up person after even a few months of college and one who resents parental intrusions.

If you would like to do more reading on the subject, a valuable reference is *Letting Go: A Parents' Guide to Today's College Experience* by K. L. Coburn and M. L. Treeger (Adler and Adler, 1988, 1992).

References

Allen, R.V. (1976). *Language experiences in communication*. Boston: Houghton Mifflin.

Bayly, J. (1972). *Psalms of my life*. Carol Stream, IL: Tyndale House.

Covington, M.V. (1992). *Making the grade: A self-worth perspective on motivation and school reform*. NY: Holt, Rinehart, and Winston.

Dobson, J. (1979, revised edition). *Hide or seek: How to build self-esteem in your child*. Old Tappan, NJ: Fleming H. Revell Co.

Dobson, J. (1999). *The new hide or seek: Building self-esteem in your child*. Grand Rapids, MI: Baker Book House.

Farris, P. (2000). *Language arts: Process, product, and assessment*. NY: Mc Graw-Hill.

Fettig, A. (1980). *Self-esteem credo*. Battle Creek, MI: Growth Unlimited, Inc.

Gardner, H. and Hatch, T. (1989). Multiple intelligences go to school. *Educational Researcher*, 18(8), 4-10.

Gardner, H. (1983). *Frames of mind: The theory of multiple intelligences*. NY: Basic.

Gardner, H. (1993). *Multiple intelligences: The theory in practice*. NY: Basic Books.

Gordon T. (1975). *Parent effectiveness training*. NY: New American Library.

Gordon, T. (2000, 30th edition). *Parent effectiveness training*. NY: Crown Publishing.

International Reading Association (2000). *Materials for parents and teachers*. Newark, DE.

Keys for kids: Daily devotionals using children's Bible hour stories. Grand Rapids, MI: Children's Bible Hour.

Kubler-Ross, E. (1969, 1991). *On death and dying*. NY: Macmillan.

Marland, S.P. (1972). *Education of the gifted and talented*. Report to Congress. Washington, D.C: U.S. Government Printing Office.

Michigan Reading Association. (1997). *What do parents want to know about early literacy programs?* Grand Rapids, MI.

Post, A.R. with M. Scott and M. Theberge (2000). *Celebrating children's choices: 25 years of children's favorite books*. Newark, DE: International Reading Association.

Prelutsky, J. (1984; 1995). *The new kid on the block*. NY: Greenwillow Books.

Prokofieff (composer), *Peter and the Wolf*. RCA Victor LM 1803 Red Seal Records, The Boston Pops Orchestra, Arthur Fiedler, Conductor, and Richard Hale, Narrator.

Routman, R. (2000). *Conversations*. Portsmouth, NH: Heinemann.

Routman, R. (1991). *Invitations*. Portsmouth, NH: Heinemann.

Shapiro, A. (1982). I speak, I say, I talk. In W.J. Smith (Ed.). *A Green Place*. NY: Delacorte.

Shapiro, A. (1997). Ill. by Tomie dePaola. *Mice squeek; we speak: A poem*. NY: Putnam.

Stauffer, R. (1970). *The language experience approach to the teaching of reading*. NY: Harper Collins.

Trelease, J. (1992). *Hey! Listen to this: Stories to read aloud*. NY: Penguin.

Trelease, J. (1993). *Read all about it! Great read-aloud stories, poems, and newspaper pieces for teens and preteens*. NY: Penguin.

Trelease, J. (1979; 1995-3rd revised edition). *The read-aloud handbook*. NY: Penguin.

U.S. Department of Education (1986). *What works: Research about teaching and learning*. Washington, D.C.

Vacca, R., Vacca, J., and Gove, M. (1987). *Reading and learning to read*. NY: Little, Brown.

Vacca, R., Vacca, J., and Gove, M. (2000). *Reading and learning to read*. NY: Addison-Wesley.

Woolfolk, A. (1980). *Educational psychology*. Needham Heights, MA: Allyn and Bacon.

Woolfolk, A. (1998). *Educational psychology*. Needham Heights, MA: Allyn and Bacon.

Sources of Information on Parents, Children, and Reading

International Reading Association, 800 Barksdale Rd., Box 8139, Newark, DE 19714-8139. 1-800-336-READ. www.reading.org (see order form on pages 191-192).

Michigan Reading Association, 5241 Plainfield Ave. N.E., Suite I, Box 10, Grand Rapids, MI 49525 1-800-MRA-READ. www.iserv.net/~mraread

Children's Book Council, Inc., P.O.Box 2640/JAF Station, New York, NY 10116-2640, www.cbcbooks.org, represents hundreds of publishers of children's books and promotes reading through the events it sponsors and the materials it produces. CBC sponsors National Children's Book Week annually in November and the Young People's Poetry Week annually in April. CBC produces a variety of materials that promote reading. Their posters can decorate bedrooms and recreation rooms. Their bookmarks make clever party favors. For a free catalog they can be reached at 1-800-999-2160.

Articles by Arden R. Post as published in *Christian Home and School* magazine

Developing Self-Esteem and Literacy in the Early Years

I Am Lovable and Capable: Developing a Positive Self-Concept, *Christian Home and School*, 64 (1), 23-25, (January 1986).

Listening: The First Step Toward Language, *Christian Home and School*, 67 (1), 20-21, (January 1989).

"I Want 'Dis' Dog"-A Child Speaks, *Christian Home and School*, 67 (2), 24-25, (February 1989).

You Weren't Listening! Untangling the Lines of Communication, *Christian Home and School*, 65 (8), 27-29, (December 1987).

Circles on the Wall: A Young Child Begins to Write, *Christian Home and School*, 67, (4), 20-21, (April 1989).

Helping Children Face Issues of Acceptance

Why Wasn't I Invited? The Birthday Party Tragedy, *Christian Home and School*, 66 (4), 24-26, (April 1988).

I Didn't Make the Team (and Other Losses), *Christian Home and School*, 69 (4), 12-15, (September 1991).

New Kids in School: Welcoming the Newcomer, *Christian Home and School*, 68 (6), 14-16, (September 1990).

The Misfit: Painful Memories from Junior High, *Christian Home and School*, 70 (4), 12-15, (September 1992).

Healing the Hurt: Teaching Kindness and Respect, *Christian Home and School*, 71(2), 16-19, (March-April 1993).

Facilitating Literacy and Learning at Home

Boosting Reading at Home, *Christian Home and School*, 63 (7), 24-25, (October 1985).

A Reading Program that Works: Sustained Silent Reading (SSR), *Christian Home and School*, 67 (3), 23-25, (March 1989).

Reading Aloud with Your Kids, *Christian Home and School*. 77(1), 18-20, (January-February 1999).

Parents and Schools: The Home-School Relationship, *Christian Home and School*, 69 (5), 12-15, (October 1991).

Scenes from a Christian School Classroom: What Makes a Christian School Christian? *Christian Home and School*, 77(4), 10-13, (September 1999).

Developing Responsibility for Life and Learning

Allowances: To Give or Not to Give: That is the Question! published as Allowances: Spare Change or Slave Wages? *Christian Home and School*, 65 (1), 22-23, (January 1987).

Raising Responsible Kids, *Christian Home and School*, 74(1), 19-21, (January-February 1996).

The Study Battle: A Necessary Tug of War? *Christian Home and School*, 63 (6), 15-17, (September 1985).

January Blahs and Homework Blues: Keeping the Momentum, *Christian Home and School*, 75(1), 16-19, (January-February 1997).

Facing Special Needs in Educating Children

Is My Child Gifted? Don't Be Afraid to Ask, *Christian Home and School*, 64 (2), 24-26, (February 1986).

No Matter How Worthy: Do Parents Have Unconditional Love? (By Arden R. Post and Karen Rigotti), *Christian Home and School*, 65 (2), 22-24, (February 1987).

Love One Another: Children with Exceptionalities, *Christian Home and School*, 63 (6), 22-24, (September 1986).

Meet David, a Disabled Reader: A Case History, *Christian Home and School*, 68, (3), 20-24, (March 1990).

Lance-LD, RD, or Just a Kid with Learning Problems? *Christian Home and School*, 68, (4), 23-26, (April 1990).

Adjusting to Changes and Challenges in Family Life

From Korea with Love: A Personal Adoption Story, *Christian Home and School*, 66 (2) 12-14, (February 1988).

Remembering Buffy: Handling the Death of the Family Pet, *Christian Home and School*, 72(6), 16-18, (December 1994).

Packing Up and Moving On: Families in Flux, *Christian Home and School*, 65 (3), 14-17, (March 1987).

Here Comes Summer! *Christian Home and School*, 64 (5), 20-22, (May-June 1986).

Letting Go: A Child Leaves for College, *Christian Home and School*, 67, (6), 19-22, (September 1989).

Christmas: 'Tis the Season to Be Jolly? *Christian Home and School*, 64 (8), 13-15, (December 1986).

Material for Parents and Teachers from the International Reading Association

The International Reading Association offers a wonderful selection of material for parents, teachers, and others interested in encouraging reading among young people. See below for details on ordering these informative brochures and booklists. To make your selection, please put a check on the corresponding line.

Parent Brochures

_____ **Library Safari: Tips for Parents of Young Readers and Explorers**
(Available in English and Spanish—please circle language choice) No. 1032-631

_____ **See the World on the Internet: Tips for Parents of Young Readers—and "Surfers"**
(Available in English and Spanish—please circle language choice) No. 1026-631

_____ **Get Ready to Read! Tips for Parents of Young Children**
(Available in English and Spanish—please circle language choice) No. 1017-631

_____ **Explore the Playground of Books: Tips for Parents of Beginning Readers**
(Available in English and Spanish—please circle language choice) No. 1019-631

_____ **Summer Reading Adventure! Tips for Parents of Young Readers**
(Available in English and Spanish—please circle language choice) No. 1023-631

_____ **Making the Most of Television: Tips for Parents of Young Viewers**
(Available in English and Spanish—please circle language choice) No. 1024-631

_____ **Make the Reading-Writing Connection: Tips for Parents of Young Learners**
(Available in English and Spanish—please circle language choice) No. 1038-631

_____ **Understanding Your Child's Learning Differences**
(Available in English and Spanish—please circle language choice) No. 1037-631

Single Copies of each parent brochure are available upon request. Send a stamped self-addressed 9 1/2 x 4 (No. 10) envelope to **Dept. E.G.**, International Reading Association, 800 Barksdale Road, PO Box 8139, Newark, DE 19714-8139 (For 1-3 titles include .34 postage; for 4-6 titles, .56 postage; and for 7-10 titles, .78 postage). **Single copies** are also available to download on-line at **bookstore.reading.org**

Bulk copies are available from the **Order Dept.** at US$15.00/100, which also includes shipping and handling charges. (**Bulk copies** price applies to 100 of the same brochure only.) All bulk orders must be prepaid. Members receive 20% off the list price.

OVER >>>>

Annotated Choices Lists

_____ **2000 Children's Choices** An annotated, illustrated list of favorite books chosen by elementary school children from across the U.S. No. 9106-631

_____ **2000 Young Adults' Choices** An annotated, illustrated list of favorites books chosen by junior and senior high school students from across the U.S. 9107-631

_____ **2000 Teacher's Choices** An annotated, illustrated list of books for all ages identified by teachers as the most helpful and enjoyable to use in the classroom. No. 9108-631

Single copies of the annotated Choices lists are available by sending a self-addressed 9 x 12 envelope to **Dept. E.G. Include US$1.00 for each list requested to cover postage and handling.** Single copies are also available to download on-line at **www.reading.org/choices**.

Bulk quantities of each annotated Choices list are available from the **Order Dept.** at the following prices:
US$9.00 for 10, which includes shipping charges
US$50.00 for 100, which includes shipping changes
US$185.00 for 500, which includes shipping charges

2000 Choices Bookmarks may be requested by sending a self-addresses (9 1/2 x 4) envelope. Your envelope should be stamped with **first-class postage.** You may request **one of each bookmark or any combination of bookmarks, limited to no more than three per request.** Bulk quantities are available for US$10.00 per 100 of each bookmark ordered.

All orders must be prepaid. Make checks payable to International Reading Association. Members receive 20% off the list price.

Order Form

Send To: _____

Address: _____

_____

$ _____ Enclosed

Mail check and form to: International Reading Association
800 Barksdale Road
PO Box 8139
Newark, DE 19714-8139